Praise

'It's great to see a book giving a practical perspective on such an important subject. David has created a powerful toolkit to support all aspects of fundraising, backed up by thorough research and narrated in an easy and extremely enjoyable style. If you are a founder thinking of fundraising or considering your next round, then it is definitely worth a read.'
— **Antonia Burridge,** Co-Founder and Director, PwC Raise Ventures

'This book is an exceptionally useful guide for female entrepreneurs wanting to know more about funding. David's knowledge of the subject and passion to level the playing field are palpable and his conversational style makes the book easy to digest. Whether you know nothing about funding and want to develop your understanding of the available options or you are already on the funding journey and want to perfect your pitch, this is a must-read book.'
— **Sophie Milliken,** award-winning serial entrepreneur

'This book opens up so many avenues for women – and all others too – seeking funding for their businesses. It is a fascinating read, filled with practical advice on how to raise money for your

business from someone with proven funding skills and successes. This is how to do it. Just read the book and go for it!'
   — **Angela Heylin LVO, OBE,** Chair (retired),
      Charles Barker plc

'As a female business owner, I learned so much reading this book. Not only about the funding landscape but also about myself. Sensitive, powerful and informative, this book will help level the playing field for many female business owners. It will change many lives.'
   — **Tammy Banks,** Co-Founder and CEO,
      Taye Training

'Entertaining, enlightening and genuinely inspiring for women founders and anyone looking to level the playing field in venture capital funding.'
   — **Maureen Sullivan,** Director of Education,
      The Procurement School

'An invaluable overview of the current bias against female founders. Despite the waste and injustice revealed in the book, the author offers practical solutions and, ultimately, hope. This is an insightful guide for anyone interested in redressing the power balance and making money.'
   — **Olivia James,** performance specialist,
      therapist, coach

FUNDED FEMALE FOUNDERS

How to traverse the uneven playing field and secure funding to grow your business

David B Horne

Also by David B Horne:

Add Then Multiply: How small businesses can think like big businesses and achieve exponential growth

R^ethink

First published in Great Britain in 2022
by Rethink Press (www.rethinkpress.com)

Cover illustrations by Jeremy Duncan

Author photograph by Clark Smith-Stanley

Front cover images licensed by Ingram Image

Contents

For Kate, Vicky and Madsie:
*'You Are the Everything'**

Foreword

I'm thrilled that David has written this book. I'm thrilled for several reasons. First of all – thank you, David, for calling your book 'Funded Female Founders'.

Why does this matter?

As you will see reading this book, venture capitalists' and investors' refusal to fund female founders is a huge, well-documented and much-covered phenomenon. The problem with the multitude of media headlines examining 'why aren't investors funding female founders?' is that those headlines make investors feel good about not funding female founders – because if everybody else isn't funding them either, it must be the right thing to not do. 'Funded Female Founders' says funding women is the right thing to do.

Second, I'm thrilled that throughout this book, David has used the default female pronoun. It's a small thing – but we notice. And it speaks volumes about any man who does that as a matter of course. That's true allyship.

Third, David's book is a terrific, practical primer for any female founder. He lays out different funding options and routes to success that counter the standardised venture capital (VC) template narrative perpetuated by the white men of Silicon Valley.

And fourth – David could not have made it clearer how much he believes in us.

Every female founder, like myself, encountered a personal problem and created a highly effective solution for it. You can extrapolate out from each of us to millions, even billions of other women – and men – who will pay for that solution. Every one of us is a unicorn in waiting. When investors haven't even begun to fund female founders at the same level as male, we have not even begun to tap into the colossal market opportunity represented by 50% of the population.

David believes in that opportunity, and I'm delighted that with this book, he's committed to helping us all achieve it.

Cindy Gallop
Founder and CEO, MakeLoveNotPorn

Introduction

The goal of this book is simple: it shows you how to traverse the uneven playing field which female founders face when raising capital. It sets out the harsh reality of an unfair marketplace and gives female founders the tools, tips and tricks to have the best chance of securing funding to grow your business. The goal is simple. That's not to say it's going to be easy.

Why is a man writing this book? Let me tell you a story.

It started with a simple question. I'm ashamed to admit this, but when I was asked the question, not only did I not know the answer, I did not even know about the issue it raised.

It was the spring of 2019 and I had been on stage, speaking about raising venture capital (VC) for small- and medium-sized enterprises (SMEs). Venture capitalists are professional investors who buy shares in companies in return for cash so those companies can grow. After my talk, a woman came over and asked me, 'Why does so little VC funding go to female entrepreneurs?'

'I have no idea,' I replied. 'But I'll find out.' The question came from a woman, let's call her 'Elizabeth' (not her real name), and I am grateful to her for opening my eyes. Once you truly see something, it cannot be unseen.

A week after appearing on that stage, I was in a meeting with the chief executive of the British Business Bank. She and I had met a few weeks previously at a networking event. We had a pleasant conversation and towards the end, I decided to ask if she knew about the lack of VC funding going to female entrepreneurs.

With a wry smile, she reached into a drawer in her desk and pulled out 'UK VC & Female Founders', a full-scale research report which the UK government commissioned the bank to prepare. Researchers looked at all the VC deals funded in the UK in 2017 and what they found was pretty stark.

Out of all the money invested by VC firms in that year, the amount going to all-female founding teams was less than 1%. These teams submitted 5% of pitch decks, but got less than 1% of total funding. That's a 1 in 5 success rate. Just 10% of funding went to mixed-gender teams, who had submitted 20% of pitch decks. A little better, but it's still only a 1 in 2 success rate. All-male teams received more than 89% of total funding, even though they only submitted 75% of pitch decks. That's 1.2 to 1.

Something is wrong here.

Not long after that meeting, I was talking to a friend who works at the London Stock Exchange, an organisation which has been leading the charge to get more women on to the boards of companies listed in the UK. She and I were discussing the 'UK VC & Female Founders' report when inspiration hit me. I felt compelled to put on an event to raise awareness about this issue – not an event that moans about how wrong or unfair it all is, but one showcasing female founders who have traversed the uneven playing field and succeeded in raising funding to grow their businesses.

A week before the event, *Morningstar* published an article which found of the almost 1,500 listed open-ended investment funds in the UK, 108 of them are run by men named David. As I'm named David, this sounded kind of cool; but wait. The same article tells us only 105 funds are run by women. More funds are run by a man called David than by all women? Something is wrong here too.

As *Morningstar* concluded, 'It's a stark reminder of the lack of diversity across the fund industry, which is often accused of being "pale, male and stale".'

On 25 November 2019, it was a full house in the theatre at the London Stock Exchange – full of entrepreneurs, investors, advisors, students and others who had come to hear the stories of women successfully raising equity funding. Two things became strikingly clear to me from this event.

First, this isn't just a UK problem. In social media posts my team and I did for the event, we received comments from people living in countries around the world – Australia, Belgium, Canada, China, France, Germany, Ireland, South Africa, Switzerland and the USA – all saying it is a big issue for them too. Second, nobody seemed to be looking at this issue from the perspective of the entrepreneur. The investment industry had put on events focused on investors, but nobody was focusing on the founders – the people who are actually facing the challenge.

This is a global issue that affects all of us. The playing field is not level. Most money is managed by men called David and the vast majority of it goes to men like him. 'Pick a David, any David' should not be the criterion on which funding is allocated.

After the success of our first event, my team and I planned to run a series of events in 2020, but a virus had other ideas and our plans were scuppered. Later in that year, we decided to run another big event, this one online, on the anniversary of the first one: 25 November. This time, we reached a global audience, stretching as far west as San Francisco, USA; as far east as Cebu, Philippines; and as far south as Cape Town, South Africa.

In 2021, we held three smaller events and the third Annual Conference in November. In March 2022, we were back at the London Stock Exchange, filling the theatre once again and streaming live to a global audience. From the events we've held so far, with little spent on marketing, we have attracted attendees from fifty-four countries on six continents. I don't think there are many entrepreneurs in Antarctica. If you know one, please share this book with them.

You may be wondering where my interest in gender equality comes from. It goes back fifty years before I met Elizabeth. In 1969, when I was seven years old, I told my mum I really loved chocolate chip cookies and wanted more. Her response?

'Let me teach you how to bake chocolate chip cookies.' Baking quickly developed into cooking, and by the time I was twelve, I was making dinner for the whole family at least once a week.

At the age of fifteen, when I met my first girlfriend, I told my mum I thought I looked much smarter wearing shirts that had been ironed.

'Simple,' she said. 'I'll teach you how to iron shirts.' In an age when baking, cooking and ironing were considered 'women's jobs', I am truly grateful my mum did not subscribe to such constraints. Learning about gender equality as a child was powerful and I'm grateful to my mum (who is ninety-three years old as I write this) for teaching this in a way that was gentle, clear and unequivocal.

My wife and I met when we were seventeen and have been together more than forty years; our daughters are twenty-nine and thirty-one. Gender equality has been the norm for me throughout my adult life, just as my mum taught me gently, clearly, unequivocally.

The numbers

Let me set out my approach to numbers and currencies in this book. Because my audience is global while the individual stories are local, I have converted all financial numbers into US dollars, so there is a single baseline for everyone. Most entrepreneurs, financiers and businesspeople I know are familiar with the exchange rate between their local currency and the greenback, so it's the easiest solution.

Now let me share with you a big number. In her landmark report, 'The Alison Rose Review of Female Entrepreneurship', NatWest Bank CEO Alison Rose determined that the economic impact to the United

Kingdom of backing female founders at the same level as male founders amounted to $350 billion, which according to the website Statista.com is 12.4% of the UK's pre-pandemic Gross Domestic Product (GDP). Also from Statista.com, the pre-pandemic GDP for the entire world was $87 trillion.

I know from my research and the interviews I have conducted that the gender funding gap is consistent in the USA, the UK and Europe. In other parts of the world, it is even bigger. Let's take the 12.4% figure from The Rose Review and adjust it down to 10% to keep the maths simple. Applying 10% to global GDP gives you eight trillion, seven hundred billion dollars. That's a really *big* number.

How big is $8.7 trillion? Let's write it out: $8,700,000,000,000. Based on NASDAQ data at the time of writing, it is more than three times the market capitalisation of Apple Inc, the largest publicly listed company in the world. It is nearly three times the value of all the unicorns in the world (private companies with a valuation of more than $1 billion) based on Crunchbase data. If it were a country, based on Statista.com data it would be the third largest in the world in terms of GDP, behind the USA and China – bigger than Japan.

That is money the investment industry is leaving on the table; money which could be used to make the world a better, fairer place; money the global economy could create, if only we were to fund female founders at the same level as their male counterparts.

In summary, we have two big problems: the unfair allocation of funds to female founders and the underrepresentation of women in the fund-management industry. And we have a huge – one might say ginormous – opportunity to create economic value by ensuring equal access to capital. It should be a no-brainer. Sadly, there is still much work to be done.

What's in the book?

Funded Female Founders is in three parts. Part One, 'Addressing The Uneven Playing Field', looks at what it's really like out there, based on published research and interviews I have conducted with female founders who have successfully raised money. It also looks at cognitive bias, which plays a large part in understanding the problem.

Part Two, 'Raising Funding For Your Business', is a how-to guide that looks at the different types of debt and equity fundraising available to entrepreneurs, from bootstrapping through to private equity. We will look at this from the perspective of a fictitious business called ABC Limited, which is run by Annabel, Briony and Charlotte. You'll meet them soon.

Part Three, 'Making Fundraising Fair', explores the economic, social and political changes that are necessary to level the playing field. It's going to be hard work, so I am dedicating the rest of my life to it. On behalf of Davids everywhere, we must level the playing field. With your help, we will.

I'll close this introduction with one of my favourite quotes:

> 'This is the true joy in life, the being used for a purpose recognized by yourself as a mighty one; the being thoroughly worn out before you are thrown on the scrap heap; the being a force of Nature instead of a feverish selfish clod of ailments and grievances complaining that the world will not devote itself to making you happy.

> 'I am of the opinion that my life belongs to the community, and as long as I live, it is my privilege to do for it whatever I can. I want to be thoroughly used up when I die, for the harder I work, the more I live. Life is no "brief candle" to me. It is a sort of splendid torch which I have got hold of for a moment, and I want to make it burn as brightly as possible before handing it on to future generations.'

> — George Bernard Shaw

PART ONE
ADDRESSING THE UNEVEN PLAYING FIELD

Part One focuses on reality at the time of writing, starting in Chapter 1 with a review of the latest statistics, research and other articles setting out the actual situation faced by female founders. Having seen how bad it really is, in Chapter 2 you will read stories of success from female founders I have interviewed. They traversed the uneven playing field and raised the capital they needed. It can be done and I hope you will be inspired by them. Chapter 3 then delves into the issue of cognitive bias, which I believe plays a significant role in causing the uneven playing field to remain.

1

What It's Really Like Out There

Before Elizabeth asked me the question, 'Why does so little funding go to female entrepreneurs?' I had no idea of the uneven playing field female entrepreneurs face when raising capital. I'm a middle-aged man. I'm one of the Davids.

I'm grateful to Elizabeth for asking me the question. She opened my eyes to a grave injustice in the world and my mind to the possibilities. The injustice is happening in fundraising, a field which – because of my life's trajectory – I know a lot about.

There is no question it's tough out there and men get most of the money. There is ample research to prove it and I will share extracts from the research with you in this chapter. The world of possibility Elizabeth opened my mind to is that I can do something about it.

All my life, I've had a soft spot for the underdog – for people who haven't been treated fairly or face an uphill struggle to achieve something. All my life, I've wanted to speak out about it. To make a ruckus about it, but I was missing the 'it'. Without the 'it', my ruckus would have been, as Shakespeare wrote in the Scottish play, '...full of sound and fury, / Signifying nothing.'

A few years ago, a friend of mine described me as an activist. I liked that, but at the same time, I thought that to be successful as an activist, I'd have to have a cause I feel passionate about. Now, dear reader, I have the cause; I have my 'it'.

In addition to the shocking statistics on the share of funding, the 'UK VC & Female Founders' report from the British Business Bank said at current rates of change, it would be 2045 before all-female teams got from the current <1% of total funding to just 10%. I'll turn eighty-three in 2045. I plan to keep at it then and beyond, although I recognise I may need others to pick up and carry the torch after I'm gone. To borrow from the late Steve Jobs, this is the dent I want to make in the universe: to level the uneven playing field.

Recently, I was attending a webinar at which four professional investors were speaking. All men. More

Davids, although none of them was named David. It was interesting when I asked them why they thought so little funding went to female entrepreneurs.

Two recognised the issue, but did not really have much to say about it, other than the VC industry was 'working on it'. The other two said it was lack of deal flow. According to them, there aren't enough opportunities pitched by female founders. It was a Zoom webinar, so sadly I could not speak to them to rebut the response; I could only post my question in the question-and-answer panel. I screamed 'That's not true!' at my computer screen, but alas, the webinar ended.

More findings from the British Business Bank

The researchers for the British Business Bank looked at the big question: why do VC firms not invest in teams with female founders? They considered two key elements to this, based on their analysis of the investment funnel.

First, they looked at the prevalence of women in both VC firms and industry. One of the issues they identified was that, while female representation in VC firms has increased from where it was ten years ago, female venture capitalists are rare, rarer still at senior levels. Across UK VC firms, only 13% of the senior investment team are women; 48% of investment teams have no women at all. There is a lot of work to be done inside the VC firms themselves.

If we turn to industry, in software companies, which attract the most VC deals, 26% of employees are female. At seniority levels across industry generally, 35% of all managerial positions are held by women. In this context, it is not surprising that the researchers found that 25% of all pitch decks submitted came from teams with at least one female member. Those pitch decks received just 11% of the investment.

Second, they looked at the interaction between female founders and VC firms. A significant element of deal flow gets to VC firms through their networks, which can be opaque. Introductions to venture capitalists often come from founders of other investee companies, angel investors (more on this subject in Chapter 6), bankers, lawyers and accountants. Where female founders are not connected into this world, they may find it significantly harder than their male counterparts to reach a VC firm.

Founders and VC firms typically connect in three ways: a warm introduction from someone in the VC firm's network; a cold approach by the founder submitting a pitch deck with no prior contact; or when they meet at an event. Warm introductions still matter in this world. The British Business Bank researchers found deals from a warm introduction were thirteen times more likely to get to the investment committee level in the VC firm and secure funding. The data supports the suggestion there is bias against female founders.

A further suggestion from the research is the perception all-male teams are the norm and all-female teams are atypical, thus representing higher risk. Indeed, the researchers found 61% of investment committees (ICs) did not consider any all-female teams, and a further 24% of ICs did not consider any all-female or mixed-gender teams. That's 85% in total who ignored teams with women in them. Women aren't even getting to the table, let alone to the funding.

Three studies from Harvard

In 2014, two professors from Harvard Business School conducted a number of field studies and drew some scary conclusions. In each case, the participants were a group of experienced angel investors or venture capitalists. Here is what the professors found:

- From a selection of pitches delivered in real competitions, male presenters had a 60% better chance of securing funding than female presenters.

- In a separate study, where the content of the pitch was the same and the presenter was talking to slides, but not visible to the investors, 68% of investors funded pitches delivered by a male voice and just 32% funded those delivered by a female voice.

- Pitches given by male voices scored over 10% more than those given by female voices in terms of persuasiveness, delivery of facts and logic.

The article concluded:

'In short, across a field setting and two experiments, there was a profound and consistent gender gap in entrepreneur persuasiveness. Investors were found to make funding decisions based on the gender and physical attractiveness of the entrepreneurs themselves.'

Another study, published in *Harvard Business Review* in 2018, looked at the impact of diversity on financial performance, after reviewing tens of thousands of VC investments and the decisions made by thousands of venture capitalists. This study delved deeply into the issue of bias, which we will address in more detail in Chapter 3. For now, let's focus on the researchers' findings in terms of the benefits of diversity.

The authors concluded:

'Diversity significantly improves financial performance on measures such as profitable

investments at the individual portfolio-
company level and overall fund returns.
And even though the desire to associate
with similar people – a tendency academics
call homophily – can bring social benefits
to those who exhibit it, including a sense of
shared culture and belonging, it can also lead
investors and firms to leave a lot of money on
the table.'

The final study, published by *Harvard Business Review* in 2020 and co-authored by Lang and Van Lee, looked at both race and gender gaps in the VC ecosystem. It reported investments made by VC firms in the United States over the previous decade had quadrupled, female-founded firms had grown to 40% of all new businesses, and businesses started by non-white founders had also grown. Despite that, the share of VC funding to female founders had barely moved since 2012, and it was even worse for Black and Latinx founders.

The current situation around the world

VC funding exploded in 2021, breaking all historic records. Stories of the 'wall of money' have been widespread, and according to Crunchbase, investment by VC firms globally hit $643 billion in 2021, up 92% on 2020. Yet again, female founders are not getting their fair share of this money.

According to Pitchbook, a total of $330 billion was invested by VCs in the USA in 2021 – up by 91% – while investments in Europe topped $120 billion – a growth of 115% over 2020. Mixed-gender teams in the USA received $56 billion, more than double the previous year, and their share of total funding in the USA grew from 12.3% to 15.6%. Funding to all-female teams was $6.4 billion, up by 84%, but as a share of total funding, it fell from 2.2% to just 2%. That's down two years in a row, after reaching 2.6% in 2019. You have to go back to 2009 to see funding to female founders at its record high of 2.8% in the USA.

Staying with Pitchbook data and moving across the Atlantic to Europe, it's an even worse story. Despite the record-breaking sums invested, the share of funding to mixed-gender teams fell from 14.4% in 2020 to 13.4% in 2021, and the share to all-female teams collapsed from 2.4% to just 1% of the total. Four years after the data published in 'UK VC & Female Founders', the needle hasn't moved.

It's not a question of deal flow, which some narrow-minded investors have told me is the reason they don't invest in female founders. As you can see from the graphic, all-male teams are submitting around 75% of decks in the USA and getting well over 80% of funding.

It's a similar story in Europe. Mixed-gender teams are holding their own, but the situation for all-female

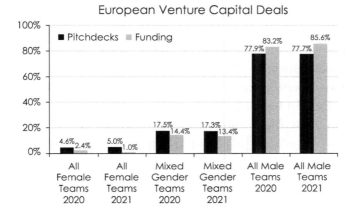

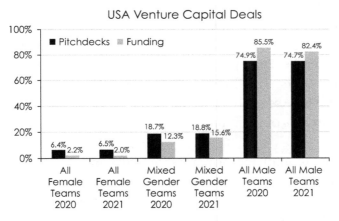

The share of funding to female founders falls again.
Source: Pitchbook

teams is getting worse. All-female teams submitted 5% of decks in Europe and 6.5% of decks in the USA – both up year-on-year – and yet their share of funding fell year-on-year to 1% in Europe and 2% in the USA.

Since 2008, in both the USA and Europe, which account for three-quarters of VC investment globally, the share of funding to female founders has never broken through 3%. My research suggests the share is even lower in much of the rest of the world. A study by Extend Ventures found that in the UK between 2009 and 2019, there were only ten Black female founders who successfully raised funding. Ten in a decade. Scandalous.

In 2019, the UK government published the Investing in Women Code. It was initially supported by fourteen organisations – ten banks, two trade associations for angel investors and two VC firms. At the end of December 2021, just eighty-seven VC firms had signed the code. The British Private Equity and Venture Capital Association has more the 325 members. More than 73% of them have not signed up.

The situation in Germany shows just under 5% growth in the number of female-founded businesses over the past five years, with the total in 2019 standing at 15.7% of all businesses, up from 13% in 2015 according to *Female Founders Monitor*. This report did not give figures for the total amount of capital raised by female-founded teams, but it did analyse the breakdown of funding by the size of deal, which was interesting.

Funding of less than $300K was secured by 75.9% of female teams and 49.3% of male teams. At the other end of the spectrum, funding of more than $1.2 million was secured by 5.2% of female teams and 27.8% of male teams. The percentage of male teams breaking the million-dollar threshold is more than five times the percentage of female teams.

An article published by *The Hindu Business Line* in 2020 reported that of the top 150 funded startups in India, less than 6.5% of the money went to firms with a female founder or co-founder. It was the lowest share in the last five years.

An article published by Which-50 Media in 2019 reported that of the $1 billion invested by VC firms in Australia and New Zealand in 2018, all-female teams received less than 3% of total funding, concluding: 'The boys' club is as entrenched as ever.'

Perhaps more worryingly, a friend recently sent me an article written by a female founder in Australia. She is a serial entrepreneur and tells the tale of meeting a wealthy investor who agreed to invest $100K in her business, but only if she would have sex with him.

Something has to change.

What about the investors?

It's a similar story when you look at the investment industry. The number of females at senior levels in VC firms is low and the VC industry is slow to change.

Successful VCs have a good life and make a great deal of money. Where is the incentive for them to change?

Authors of an article published in *Harvard Business Review* looked at the data on every USA-based VC firm and its investors over the period 1990–2018. They found the percentage of female investors was relatively steady across the entire twenty-eight-year period, at just 8%. Three-quarters of VC firms in the United States had never hired a female investor. A separate study from *Women in VC* found just 4.9% of partners in VC firms were women. The *Harvard Business Review* article also found VC firms which increased the number of female partners by 10% were achieving incremental returns of 1.5% per annum on their investment portfolio and 9.7% more profitable exits.

An article published by Boston Consulting Group reported female-led firms generated 2.5 times as much revenue per dollar invested as male-led firms, so why are investors not flocking towards female-led businesses? This is a massive missed opportunity, both for the investors who are failing to tap into higher returns and for the successful women who want to raise funds and grow their businesses.

Chapter wrap

We've covered a lot of statistics and numbers in this chapter, and you may be feeling down about just how bad the situation really is regarding investment in female-founded businesses. Fear not, we'll be looking at opportunities in the next chapter. It's best to get the bad news out of the way so we can concentrate on the positives in the rest of this book.

Fundraising is hard work for everyone. It's a full-time job on top of the day job of running a business. The statistics in this chapter show – in many countries around the world, over an extended period – female founders face an uneven playing field when it comes to raising capital. Globally, it seems the funding ceiling to female founders is sitting around 3%, yet women make up 51% of the world's population.

This gives a powerful indication of just how uneven the playing field is, particularly in light of women outperforming men by 2.5 times in terms of revenue generated to capital invested.

There is much work to be done.

2

Success Stories From Funded Female Founders

Since discovering the shocking truth about the massive lack of funding to female entrepreneurs, I have interviewed several dozen women who have raised capital to grow their businesses. In this chapter, I share with you seven stories in the hope you will find inspiration from these women who have traversed the uneven playing field and secured funding.

This first story comes from two young women who pivoted their original proposition and pitched an idea to disrupt the market.

FIONA LEE, POD FOODS

Fiona is co-founder of Pod Foods, a logistics-enabled business-to-business (B2B) marketplace connecting retailers and brands.

Pod Foods started in San Francisco and is now headquartered in Austin.

Fiona is Singaporean Chinese and an immigrant to the United States, so the cards were stacked against her. She looks different, sounds different and clearly is not 'from around here'. She and her co-founder Larissa Russell were trying to raise money to grow a startup vegan cookie business when they realised the wholesale food distribution system in the USA is hugely skewed against small and emerging brands, and it was a massive challenge for these brands to get a break and secure distribution onto retail shelves.

After pitching to many angels and early-stage investors in Silicon Valley, they secured a follow-up meeting with a partner from a VC firm focused on supporting immigrant entrepreneurs who have pre-revenue pre-product companies in the USA. The evening before they were due to pitch, they pulled an all-nighter to document as much as possible the outline for their new distribution system and why it would be a success.

They said, 'Forget the cookie company. Look at this. This is how we are going to disrupt a market. This is how we're going to create a billion-dollar company.' In their pitches, Fiona and Larissa kept saying, 'We are going to build this – with or without you. We'd rather do it with you.'

It was a successful pivot and a successful pitch. After a few months of discussions, the partner invested enough for Fiona and Larissa to build a minimum viable product and demonstrate traction in the market.

Fiona said the initial equity stake to their investment partner was more than she and Larissa had anticipated, although she has no regrets about the decision to proceed. The investment team were with them every step of the way and supported two young, inexperienced entrepreneurs with a big idea. Pod Foods has since raised $16 million and their initial partner remains one of the cornerstone investors.

Using the funding, Fiona, Larissa and their team have built the operations of Pod Foods to simplify the supply chain from food manufacturer to retailer. They partner with logistics companies to handle fulfilment so they can concentrate on allowing startup food businesses the same opportunity to get into retailers and make their products available to consumers at the best price possible. Pod Foods is now present in ten American states, serving cities like Chicago, New York, Los Angeles and Austin, carrying over 3,500 products and delivering them to retailers across the United States.

I'm not saying it's right, but in the current climate, it is sometimes necessary for female founders to take a more aggressive stance. This was true for the successful female founder in the next story.

MAY AL-KAROONI, GLOBECHAIN

May is founder of Globechain, a multi-award-winning reuse marketplace which connects enterprises to non-profits and businesses to redistribute unneeded fixtures, products and furniture, while at the same time generating environmental, social and governance (ESG) data on the impact.

It was when she was working at an investment bank in London that the idea for Globechain came to her. Her then employer was moving to new offices across the road and simply threw away the fixtures, furnishings and everything else from the old office and bought everything new for the new office. May wondered why no one had digitised waste and could see just how wrong this was and how important it was to do something and make a change.

For four years, May self-funded the business on her own before securing seed investment (early-stage investment in a startup company) of $1 million in 2019. She recalls during the fundraising process one investor challenged her on whether she could achieve the goals set out in her business plan.

'Look what I've done for four years on my own,' she replied. 'Imagine what I could do with a team.' She had to put herself into a particular frame of mind to rebut these comments – to her, it felt arrogant, yet for men, it would have been perceived as confident.

Also comments from VCs (male and female) were ingrained and focused on asking retention questions rather than potential questions. For example, how will you retain clients, to how are you going to achieve the 20% market? She also noticed she was required to bring in a higher monthly recurring revenue (MRR) than her male counterparts.

Today, Globechain is the largest reuse marketplace in the world, with over 10,000 members and operations in the UK, Spain, the United Arab Emirates and the USA. May's mission is to divert 100 million tonnes from landfill by 2025.

Our third story shows how one woman brought together three co-founders to build a successful business employing more than 370 people.

NAN WILLIAMS, FOUR COMMUNICATIONS

Nan is co-founder and group CEO of Four Communications, one of the most successful startup communications companies with offices in the UK and the Middle East.

Nan started Four Communications with three colleagues (hence the name Four) in late 2000. She had a clear plan of what she wanted to achieve, and knew she needed funding to get the business up and running as quickly as possible. She decided the fastest and easiest way to get money was to sell her home and put the proceeds into the business. Nan is a single mother with two sons, and they moved from a big house to an apartment so she could put the seed funding into Four Communications.

It proved to be a wise move.

The company grew quickly, to start with organically, and after a few years, Nan and the team decided to make acquisitions to accelerate their growth. The initial deals were share-for-share exchanges with minimal cash outlay and deferred consideration (the portion of the price agreed, but not paid until later) funded from company profits. Once they'd completed a number of deals in this manner, the board of the company decided they had the size and scale to take on a substantial investor who would provide a war chest to make larger acquisitions.

After the usual roadshow of presentations to investors, Nan and the team agreed a deal on a $14 million investment plus a $7 million credit facility from their bankers. Over the next several years, they made large acquisitions to strengthen the group's position in its chosen markets. Today, Four offers an integrated approach with services spanning advertising, creative, branding, public relations, public affairs, behaviour change, media planning, media buying, marketing, performance, social analytics, content, web, digital marketing, video and animation, search engine optimisation, events, crisis management, corporate social responsibility, sponsorship, partnerships and training.

From a launch with three co-founders and three staff, Nan has grown Four to more than 370 people operating from six offices in the UK and the Middle East.

What about an entrepreneur whose offering is somewhat niche? This next story holds the answer.

DR DANIELA MARINO, CUTISS

Daniela is co-founder and CEO of CUTISS AG, a Swiss biotech specialising in the development of personalised skin transplant products primarily for the treatment of burns and other skin defects.

Daniela was born and raised in Sicily and decided at the age of three she wanted to be a paediatrician. That changed to science at age eight, and when she went to university in Milan, it was for a master's degree in biotechnology. Daniela completed her PhD at ETH Zurich, and during her post-doctoral research at University of Zurich (UZH), she decided to launch CUTISS.

She and the team at UZH had just secured a $6 million EU grant, which included a course on business planning in Nice, France. Daniela won the pitching competition on the course, but on the drive home from Nice to Zurich, she grappled with a dilemma: stay or go? After sleeping on it, Daniela decided to launch the company, go for equity funding and grow CUTISS as a business.

Two months after setting up, she gave birth to her second son (the first was born during the grant writing at UZH). Two months later, she launched a seed round and raised the first million. Since then, Daniela has raised $39 million in equity – the $1 million seed round in 2017, followed in 2018 by $11 million and $27 million in 2020 at the height of the pandemic. Daniela's investors are angels and family offices (more on family offices in Chapter 7); she bypassed VC entirely.

With this funding, Daniela has scaled her team to forty people and invested in both the technology behind her business's personalised skin tissue therapies and the regulatory compliance it needs to commercialise them. Its main product, denovoSkin™, is completing phase 2 trials and received 'orphan medicinal product' (a product to treat rare life-threatening or very serious conditions) status by EU, US and Swiss healthcare regulators. CUTISS recently launched the world's first personalised skin-making machine, which could have a huge impact for the millions of people who suffer severe burns every year and cannot be properly treated for lack of skin.

Daniela believes scientists have a powerful combination of visionary and methodical skills which makes them excellent CEOs. She is an advocate for girls and women studying and building careers in science and entrepreneurship.

Staying in the world of healthcare, albeit with completely different products, let's cross the ocean from Europe to Canada and hear from a serial entrepreneur.

STACEY WALLIN, CAIN

Stacey has been active on the Canadian tech scene since the beginning of her career, originally as a licensed financial professional in early-stage financings focused on growth stocks in the public markets. After founding her first business, a health-tech company that predicts and prevents workplace injuries using sensor arrays and machine learning called LifeBooster, she then led a team at BC Tech that designed scale and growth accelerator programming for entrepreneurs in her province. During this time, she also drove systemic change around equitable access in the tech sector as a subject matter expert for government projects, a speaker and community leader. Stacey was also involved in guiding policy on equitable fundraising and access to capital, where she analysed each step of the fundraising process from the perspective of the venture capitalist with a view to identifying unconscious bias. She looked at the venture capitalist's own fundraising process with its limited partners as well as the investment process, from deal sourcing to investment committee and beyond.

Towards the end of that chapter, she founded the Canadian Accelerator/Incubator Network (CAIN), since bringing together more than 140 innovation organisations in Canada with a shared interest in fair access for everyone and an intelligent look at diversity and inclusion, notably through embodying best practices and the launch of a national working group.

Stacey was also co-founder and Chief Strategy Officer of Numinus, a wellness business combining the latest advances in psychedelic medicine with the best in evidence-based care and a holistic, integrated approach to healing. The company has a licensed laboratory for conducting primary research and developing intellectual property (IP), a team developing psychedelic-assisted therapeutic protocols to embed in mainstream healthcare, as well as training and support for medical practitioners to ensure best-in-class treatment at their network of clinics in North America. Numinus has raised over $70 million and is listed on the Toronto Stock Exchange (TSX: NUMI).

When asked what advice she would give to her younger self, Stacey replied, 'Be kinder to yourself. You are learning. Seed investors are partners in your business. They can be your greatest ally or your heaviest anchor. Choose them carefully and do not compromise on your values. Only engage with those that support your diversity.'

Sexism isn't the only form of prejudice some female entrepreneurs have to deal with. Our next successful founder also had to face up to racism and homophobia.

LAUREN LEWIS, GLASSWORKS LONDON

Lauren Lewis was born in New York City and grew up in rural Pennsylvania. She returned to the Big Apple to study at Columbia and began her career in investment banking and private equity. Lauren has worked in Tokyo and Dubai, and now lives in London where she founded Glassworks London. It is a fresh British brand, showcasing images of success based around women.

During her years as a global investment banker, Lauren raised billions of dollars for clients. To succeed in a male-dominated industry, Lauren had to stay laser focused on the job in hand, always going above and beyond, and working hard to be seen as indispensable. Despite this, she experienced overt prejudice towards women, racial minorities and members of the LGBTQ++ community – and she is from all three of them. Lauren is a gay African American woman who has experienced all manner of prejudice, from petty ignorance to outright harassment.

Soon after launching Glassworks London, Lauren found herself back on the fundraising trail, completing multiple rounds of debt and equity raises. As an experienced investment banker turned entrepreneur, Lauren agreed to share her top three tips for fundraising:

- Ask yourself seriously whether you need external capital or not. Taking on an equity investor is the beginning of a long-term relationship. Some successful entrepreneurs own 100% of their companies. Can you get there on your own?

- Network. This was a new one for Lauren because her network in investment banking was not what she needed to raise startup and scale-up funding. Cold calling is tough in any industry, but in VC, it is not effective. To succeed, you must network yourself into VC firms. If you can't do that, it would suggest you do not have the tenacity to grow a business.

- Be confident in yourself and your abilities. Don't look to investors to give you permission to move forward or build the company for you. That is not their role; it's yours. Work with your investors. Find out how you can set them up for success.

Lauren believes strongly there is a huge opportunity for people who understand the scale of the funding gap to completely revolutionise the VC industry.

Finally, let's meet a successful female founder who recognised opportunity where others did not.

AGNÈS PETIT, MOBBOT

Agnès is founder and CEO of Mobbot, a construction tech startup in Switzerland which 3D prints concrete elements for sustainable infrastructure. The company develops and operates automated robotic 3D-concrete printing platforms which enable contractors to produce finished concrete pieces in an hour or two, compared with several days using the traditional methods from the concrete industry.

Agnès has spent her entire career in the construction industry, travelling the world with big cement companies and working across the whole range of business areas, from commercial management to operations. She knows the industry well and knows it has a reputation for being slow to adopt new technologies.

Her first exposure to 3D printing came when she was still employed by others, but she saw the potential where they did not. She left her employer and took time to plan out the Mobbot journey before launching the company in 2018. During the early years, she had three approaches from potential investors, each of which she turned down. The first was from a VC who offered her $250K for 49% of the company, saying she could focus time on her family life as well as the company and basically wanting to come in and take over. She said no because it went against her entrepreneurial spirit. The VC came back a year later, offering $1 million for 45% of the company. She said no again, went home and cried for the evening. I mention this because it's important for readers to understand raising finance can be an emotional rollercoaster and it's OK to ride that wave.

Agnès decided to bootstrap the business (more on bootstrapping in Chapter 6) and invest her own money in the early stages of development. She applied to startup competitions and raised finance through loans and two angel investors who trusted her idea and future plans. She developed the technology from scratch and filed the first patent for the 3D printing process in 2018. Mobbot won its first large commercial contract in the summer of 2019.

Around this time, Agnès entered extended discussions with a potential investor, but the term sheet (investment offer setting out the detailed terms) did not express trust towards her as founder nor did it reflect fair conditions for the Swiss market. It was like everything she had been discussing with the investor was no longer relevant. She turned down the third offer, went home and cried for the whole weekend. She felt disappointed and wondered if anyone would ever trust her. I'm grateful to Agnès for sharing her vulnerability so others who face this emotional challenge can learn from her experience and know they are not alone.

In 2020, Agnès found investors who were a good fit for Mobbot, her and the team. She raised $3 million in seed funding and is focusing on growing the team, which she says is now her biggest challenge.

Chapter wrap

At the end of Chapter 1, I promised we would look at the positives and the opportunities in this chapter. You have heard stories from seven female founders in seven industries and four countries who have all successfully raised funding to grow their companies. Each of them has shared their experience of fundraising and given tips and suggestions on how to do it. They have shared some of their challenges too.

My goal in this chapter was to show you it is possible: there are women who have successfully traversed the uneven playing field and raised capital – in some cases, well into eight figures – to grow their businesses. If you're feeling down and need a little inspiration, please come back to this chapter and read their stories again. It can be done. These are just seven stories. There are many more female entrepreneurs who have succeeded.

3
Cognitive Bias

There is no question. The hard statistics and the first-hand stories both show that there is bias against female entrepreneurs. While I acknowledge some men are misogynists, I would like to think for most investors, the reason for this is rather less malicious: cognitive bias driving the skew away from women.

Cognitive bias is not my area of speciality, so I am grateful to Dr Itiel Dror, who has a PhD from Harvard University specialising in human cognition, bias, expert decision making and learning, and is today senior researcher at University College London. Dr Dror has shared his knowledge and wisdom, and kindly given me permission to include some of his work in my book. As much of Dr Dror's work is focused on bias in the criminal justice sector, I have made my own interpretations as to how his findings are relevant to investing in female founders. Any errors or misinterpretations of Dr Dror's work are mine alone.

To apply cognitive bias in the field of fundraising and female entrepreneurs, and to do so with a level of academic rigour, I am grateful to Dr Dana Kanze, who has a PhD from Columbia Business School specialising in gender differences in venture financing and is today an associate professor at London Business School. Dr Kanze has given an outstanding TEDx talk, 'The real reason female entrepreneurs get less funding', and has published many peer-reviewed articles in her subject area.

Cognitive bias – an overview

It is generally accepted that scientists and other experts act impartially, drawing any conclusions they arrive at based on observable quantifiable data. This acceptance focuses on the data and methodology, not the human being making the decision on how to interpret the results, yet studies, academic and otherwise, have shown cognitive bias exists in many domains. It has an impact on how people observe, tabulate and analyse the data, as well as how they reach conclusions.

The impact of bias is not only relevant to the conclusions people draw, but also to the inputs which led to the data being produced in the first place – what data is captured or discarded as irrelevant; the strategy and execution of the testing; how it is carried out and by whom. We have seen, for example, the significant underrepresentation of women in senior roles in VC firms. There is no question this has an impact on bias.

In most cases, bias is unintentional and occurs without the person displaying it even being aware of it. Blissful ignorance, one might say. This needs to change.

Eight sources of bias

The figure on the next page sets out graphically the eight sources of bias, which can be grouped into three categories:

- Category A shows bias related to a specific case.

- Category B shows bias from the person doing the work, as opposed to anything to do with the specific case.

- Category C shows bias from human nature and the architecture of the human brain. Every one of us on the planet shares this category.

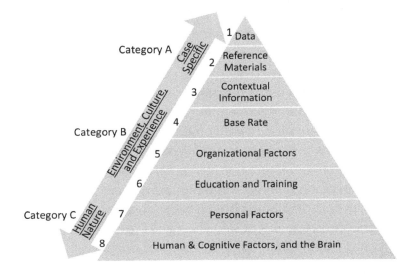

The eight sources of bias.
Copyright Dr Itiel E Dror, used with permission.

Let's briefly explore these eight sources:

Data – here, it is a case of what the actual data is and how it gets analysed. In many cases, there is no bias from the data, although it can contain potentially biasing information. In the context of funding female founders, I believe this is not a main driver of bias.

Reference materials – this source is all about how reference materials can bias how data is interpreted. Rather than relying solely on the data, the person analysing it will make assumptions as to which data may or may not be relevant to the situation at hand, based on other reference materials. Throughout society, many reference materials are blatantly gender biased, starting with children's literature.

Contextual information – this arises when contextual information not relevant to the task at hand causes bias. A great example of this would be a female founder in a male-dominated industry, like construction. Remember the challenges Agnès Petit of Mobbot raised in the previous chapter. For some people, the combination of female founder and construction industry simply doesn't stack up and they fail to see an opportunity.

Base rate – this refers to the impact previous cases may have on the analysis of a new case. Rather than the observer taking each case on its merit, base rate bias causes their decisions to be influenced by previous cases that they might consider similar. This bias can be especially strong if the similarity to previous cases is superficial or the person making the decision acts on what happened in the past rather than on the facts of the case at hand.

Organisational factors – these can be any of many factors which bias the results of an investigation, including time and budget pressures, the expectation of reaching certain results and providing what the boss wants to see. Dr Dror's studies of this in the criminal justice sector have found clear evidence that organisational factors induce bias.

Education and training – this refers to the provision of education and training to staff carrying out a particular investigation. In the case of forensic examiners, do they see their training and the work they do as supporting the police or as scientists investigating data?

Personal factors – there are many personal factors which can influence bias, including motivation, ideology and beliefs, and a person's attitude to risk or ambiguity. Evidence has shown when a person plays a key role in collecting, sampling and interpreting data, personal factors can influence the way they carry out the work and interpret the results.

Human and cognitive factors, and the brain – the workings of the human brain create structural constraints which do not allow it to process all the incoming information it receives. The brain engages in a variety of processes to make sense of the world we live in and the data we retrieve from it; it is not a camera.

The unknown unknown

As former US Defence Secretary Donald Rumsfeld famously said, 'There are known knowns... there are unknown knowns... there are also unknown unknowns.'

In the vast majority of cases, cognitive bias is an unknown unknown – the people acting in this manner are not aware of what they are doing.

As an illustration, the first time I met Dr Dror was at an event where we were both speaking. He showed a short film to the audience, asking them to pay particular attention to a group of people passing a basketball and to count the number of times it was passed from one person to the next. In the middle of the film, a person dressed in a gorilla suit entered the scene and took the ball away, before leaving the stage and tossing the ball back into the group of players. When the film was over, a show of hands proved the vast majority of the audience had not seen the gorilla.

Applying cognitive bias to the world of fundraising

Here I turn to the work of Dr Dana Kanze. Her work on implicit gender bias has been influenced by a psychological theory called regulatory focus, which was developed by Columbia University Professor E Tory Higgins. Regulatory focus differentiates between two distinct motivational orientations: promotion and prevention. As Professor Higgins notes, 'The promotion focus is concerned with accomplishments, hopes and aspirations.... The prevention focus is concerned with safety, responsibilities and obligations.'

To bring this theory to life, Dr Kanze analysed every pitch from the TechCrunch Startup Battle in New York City dating back to 2010. She found no material differences in the way male and female entrepreneurs pitched their businesses. She then turned to the question-and-answer session following each pitch, in which prospective investors asked questions of the entrepreneurs. Here, she found a huge disparity.

The table below sets out examples of promotion and prevention themes across six common areas of questioning.

	Promotion	Prevention
Customers	Acquisition	Retention
Market	Size	Share
Income statement	Sales	Margins
Balance sheet	Assets	Liabilities
Projections	Growth	Stability
Strategy	Vision	Execution

From her detailed analysis, she determined 67% of questions asked of male entrepreneurs used promotion terminology – eg 'Tell me how you are going to grow your market penetration' – and 66% of questions asked of female entrepreneurs used prevention terminology – eg 'Tell me how you are going to protect the customers you have from the competition'. Drilling further into the data, Dr Kanze looked at the types of questions asked by male and female investors, assuming female investors would ask more promotion questions of female entrepreneurs. This was not the case. In fact, both male and female investors showed the same bias in their questioning.

What was most revealing in her research was the way the entrepreneurs chose to answer the questions. Many people naturally responded in kind, giving a promotion answer to a promotion question and a prevention answer to a prevention question. This perpetuates the cycle of inherent gender bias. However, Dr Kanze found that entrepreneurs who responded to prevention questions with promotion answers went on to raise fourteen times as much funding as those who responded in kind. Fourteen times as much. That's huge. It's like politicians who never answer the question they are asked, but reply with the party line or whatever message they want to get across.

This is a key learning for entrepreneurs, especially the 66% of female entrepreneurs who are asked prevention questions. No matter which type of question you're asked, give a promotion response.

In her recent research, Dr Kanze found conclusive evidence showing female founders are penalised by investors for lack of industry fit. That is to say, female founders in industries which are traditionally male dominated (think Agnès Petit of Mobbot) receive less funding and lower valuations than female founders in traditionally female-dominated industries. Dr Kanze found no evidence to show the same applying to male founders, whether they are in traditionally male or female industries.

Chapter wrap

Gender bias is alive and well. I'm sure this will come as no surprise to the women reading this book.

Rather more alarming is how insidious bias is. We have seen from Dr Itiel Dror's research there are eight sources of bias and they are not mutually exclusive. We have seen from Dr Dana Kanze's research how this plays out in the types of questions asked of female entrepreneurs, and the significant impact it has on the level of funding they secure and the valuation at which it is secured.

The playing field is uneven. Let's see what we can do to level it up.

PART TWO
RAISING FUNDING FOR YOUR BUSINESS

In Part Two, we'll begin with an important question in Chapter 4 and close with some guidance in Chapter 8 to ensure you have the best possible chance to raise funding. In between, in Chapters 5–7, I'll take you through the main types of funding available to entrepreneurs. To make it more personal, I have created a story about a new company, ABC Limited, and its three co-founders. Let me introduce you to them.

Annabel, Briony and Charlotte met in a Zoom breakout room at an online conference. The Zoom algorithm randomly placed the three of them together; it was one of those chance encounters which ended up having a significant impact on their lives.

Annabel, twenty-seven, is a single mum who has recently been made redundant from her corporate job. She has an incredible idea for an innovative product for home-office workers. After years in a big-company job, she's excited her pioneer spirit has a chance to be set free.

Briony has just turned eighteen. Her parents are mixed heritage, which was tough for her growing up. Unable to fit in with either community as a kid, she turned to computers for solace. She is a creative genius who loves making hardware and software.

Charlotte is a retired sales executive with a background in office technology products. She is a grandmother and an accomplished drummer.

They got on so well, they decided to share contact details. Before long, they met up again in person. Annabel told the others about her idea for a tech device with wide consumer attraction which could also be used in the B2B sector. As she was telling them about it, Briony started sketching out what the product might look like. Inspired by Steve Jobs, Briony knew it was important the product looked and felt cool. She knew she had the coding skills to write the software for the prototype and at this early stage was already thinking about the design.

Charlotte sat back, watching and listening while tapping a blues rhythm on her left thigh. Briony had produced several sketches which Annabel commented on, and together they made a few tweaks and changes. It was upon seeing the fourth sketch that Charlotte finally leaned forward and spoke.

'That's the one. I can sell that.' A new startup was born.

What's really interesting is that each of them came with a specific skillset which would be of critical importance to the business. Annabel had the idea, and she understood the details of operational excellence and customer service from her corporate job, but she had no knowledge of how to build the device and had never sold anything in her life. Briony and Charlotte brought the missing skills. In other words, they each had strengths and weaknesses. Collectively, they would become a disruptive force in a fast-growing market.

They each agreed to take the title co-founder. They registered a company, ABC Limited, and each took one-third stake in the business. It was a true partnership.

4

Do You Really Want To Raise Money?

Before we dive into the details of the different funding available, I want to pose a serious question. Do you really want to raise money? It might seem a strange question to ask in a book which is substantially about fundraising. Please bear with me on this one, because in my years in business, I have found some people for whom raising money just doesn't work.

Let's have a look at a couple of the types of people I mean.

The equity hoarder

One of the most challenging discussions I have with entrepreneurs relates to their reluctance to 'give away equity'. It's an expression which bugs me, because it puts an immediate limit on their ability to achieve exponential growth.

This is a mindset thing. Something tells these entrepreneurs they must be in complete control of their business, which means they must be in complete control of the equity. It doesn't have to be the case.

Let me set the record straight here: equity should never be given away. Equity is the entrepreneur's most valuable currency. By all means exchange it for something of equal or greater value, but *never* give it away.

Please take time to make sure you have a clear understanding of this concept. For some, it comes easily. For others, it's really hard to grasp because it flies in the face of being in charge of their own destiny. It may require a complete 180 degree turn in the way you think about your business. Your brain can handle it.

Let me reiterate two points that are fundamental to everything else we are going to talk about:

1. Equity is the entrepreneur's most valuable currency.

2. By all means exchange equity for something of equal or greater value, but *never* give it away.

It's similar when people talk about their stake being diluted if a company issues more shares. If they don't want their percentage holding to reduce, then they can follow their investment and buy more shares when they are issued. Paradoxically, if the value of the shares has gone up, the value of their holding has too, even if their percentage stake decreases.

I like to use the analogy of a pie. It's all a question of how big the pie is *and* how big your slice is. The equity hoarder struggles with others having a slice, regardless of the size of the pie. Let's explore this in a little more detail.

Let's say your company is worth $3 million and you want to raise $2 million in funding. After the investor's money is put in, the company is worth $5 million (the $3 million value plus the $2 million cash). There's a subtle shift in wording here. Did you notice it?

The company now has a value of $5 million. You own 60% of it, which is the $3 million it was worth before you raised the money. The investor owns 40% of it, which is the $2 million she paid in, in return for equity.

You didn't give it away, did you? You sold it. You're still the holder of the larger percentage of shares and on a day-to-day basis you're likely to call the shots. You're probably the founder as well, and that will never change. Steve Jobs was always the founder of Apple, even when he got fired by the board and left the company.

Let's stick with the company that's now worth $5 million and take a further example. Let's talk about stock options. These are often used to attract and retain key employees. You grant an option to a key member of staff, say a new chief technology officer (CTO) for a growing tech business, which gives them the right (but not the obligation) to buy shares in the company at a date in the future, based on a price you set up front in the option agreement. If the CTO chooses to exercise the option, she will pay the agreed price in return for shares in the company. If she doesn't exercise the option, it will lapse and nothing happens.

Let's say she does exercise the option, which allows her to buy 5% of the equity in the company. In this case, you and your investor each get diluted by 5%. Now the ownership is:

- You own 57% (95% of the 60% you held previously).

- The investor owns 38% (95% of the 40% she held previously).

- The CTO owns 5%.

Did you give away any equity here? No, you sold equity in the form of an option to attract and retain the services of a CTO who will be critical to the future growth of the company, and she paid money into the company in exchange for the shares. You exchanged equity for something of equal or greater value.

We'll fast forward a few years and assume the company is now worth $10 million thanks to the great strategy you executed, funded by the investor and developed by the CTO. Your stake in the business is worth $5.7 million. The investor's stake is worth $3.8 million and the CTO's stake is worth $500,000. You and the investor have nearly doubled your money. You don't own 100% of the company and you don't control everything, but your shares in the company have increased in value from $3 million to $5.7 million.

Give away equity? I don't think so. You made smart decisions which have increased your net worth by 90%. Your slice of the pie is a lot bigger than the pie you had all of before you raised the initial funding. The investor and the CTO have also benefited, so it's win-win-win.

Think about this carefully if you are an equity hoarder.

The frugal leader

When you're starting out in business, it is important to keep a close eye on your spending. As the business grows, you must continue to do so, but one of the common types of entrepreneur I come across is the frugal leader. They don't like spending money. At all.

Now don't get me wrong; I'm not suggesting you should become profligate, but one of the key things you need to get your head around is that growth devours cash. To grow your business, you're going to need to spend money – on growing and up-skilling your team; investing in technology and marketing; as well as other overheads associated with a growing company.

In 2005, I was the chief financial officer (CFO) of a company listed on London's Alternative Investment Market. The founder and I were doing the rounds with our institutional investors after releasing our year-end financial report. One of our larger shareholders was also the largest shareholder of a competitor of ours. This shareholder was tired of the CEO of that company hoarding cash (it had $14 million in the bank and the CEO refused to spend it on growth, dividends or buying back shares) and he encouraged us to take a closer look at the company. This led to us acquiring the business and firing the management team who were running a listed company with a frugal mindset.

Your investors know growth devours cash, so you need to be comfortable with spending it. You are raising money from investors to scale the company. Don't behave like a frugal leader and risk not achieving your dreams.

What kind of business are you running?

During my years in business, I have come across many companies in many different industries and countries. I group them into four categories, which can be both destinations and points along the journey:

Solopreneur – a huge number of businesses revolve around one key person. They may be supported by external admin, bookkeeping and other business services, but it's all about one person. When they are working, the business is doing well. When they aren't working, there is no money coming in. The business might or might not be incorporated, and growth is limited by the solopreneur's time.

Lifestyle business – this type of business typically revolves around four key people to drive the core functions: sales and marketing, which is all about finding and winning customers; operations, which is all about delivering the product or service to customers; finance, which is all about managing the flow of money into and out of the company and dealing with fiscal and statutory compliance; and a visionary leader who is the face of the company and is responsible for the brand, culture and direction of the business, working with the rest of the team. Lifestyle businesses typically do not grow beyond fifteen employees, but they can be very profitable and are run to finance the owner's lifestyle.

Growth business – these businesses typically employ more than twenty-five people. One of the biggest challenges in getting to that size and scale is making the structural changes to the business to support and enable growth. It's one thing to be a co-owner of a business with a dozen people where everyone knows everyone else; it's another thing entirely to be a co-owner of a business employing, say, eighty-five people. There will be a much clearer delineation of responsibilities. There will be departments, politics and internal rivalry.

These things may also exist in a lifestyle business, but they will be alive and thriving in a growth business. There will be systems, policies and procedures. If you're the leader of the business, you might not know everyone by their first name. This is where a business can become big and successful, but it's a different kind of work running a growth business compared to being a solopreneur or running a lifestyle business.

Large business – these businesses tend to be defined as having more than 250 employees. In many cases, the original owners of the company have sold their stakes and the new owners will bring in professional management teams to run the business. Management may have an element of equity in their compensation, but in most cases, it is not more than 1–2% of the total equity.

In terms of your ability to raise capital, for solopreneurs, it's really a case of debt funding. Unless it's an exceptional circumstance, equity investors are not going to back a solopreneur. There is too much risk and the potential for high growth is not there.

For lifestyle businesses, the challenge lies in the name. The founder will often legitimately put significant personal expenses through the company's books for tax purposes, but in reality, they are not normal business expenses. There may be an opportunity for some equity funding, but smart investors will want to know the personal expenses will no longer be going through the books. Their investment is to grow the company, not to help fund the owner's lifestyle. There may be circumstances where equity funding is available to lifestyle businesses, but it would be much more common to see these funded by debt, if needed.

It is with growth businesses and startups which aim to be growth businesses where serious amounts of funding will be relevant, and this is where equity funding really kicks in. If you want to raise equity funding, it is imperative you present your company as a growth business.

Chapter wrap

Fundraising is not for everyone. Some entrepreneurs are not willing to relinquish any control. Others want to keep their businesses within the lifestyle range. Many are happy working as solopreneurs. As long as it is a strategic decision the owner(s) have made, that's cool. It's just those businesses will find it difficult to raise equity funding to finance growth.

If you're an equity hoarder or a frugal leader and you want to raise capital, you will need to change some of your thinking. If you succeed in changing your thinking, the next chapters will explore some of the opportunities that will become available to you.

5
Debt Funding

We start the fundraising section with debt. Not because it's the first step most entrepreneurs take, but because debt funding is different to equity funding, which the remaining chapters of Part Two will be covering.

What is debt funding?

There are many ways to borrow money, and with the tightening of regulation on banks and the growth of FinTech companies, there are new players entering the debt-funding market all the time. Nonetheless, the fundamental concept of debt funding remains the same: the lender lends money to the borrower and they agree a structure by which the borrower will repay the money, plus interest. The lender may also take security over assets of the company or assets of the owner(s) of the company, referred to as a personal guarantee (PG). In the event the borrower fails to repay the loan, the lender can take these assets and use or sell them to service the debt.

Over the course of my career, I have completed debt facilities from as small as $200 to as large as $14 million, and in total I have raised more than $50 million of debt funding in the UK, USA, Germany and Canada.

RAISING DEBT AT AGE FOURTEEN

The first time I raised debt, I was fourteen years old. I grew up in Canada, and in the summer of 1976, Canada hosted the summer Olympic games in Montreal. I had recently taken up coin collecting as a hobby and the Royal Canadian Mint came out with a commemorative coin set celebrating the Olympics. I wanted that set for my collection. It cost $300 and I only had $100 in savings.

I remember talking with my dad about this. He said he would take me to see his bank manager to talk about getting a loan so I could buy the coins. Dad explained to me how loans worked: I would have to make monthly repayments and there was an interest charge to pay as well. We made an appointment with the manager (back when banks actually had branch managers who made loans, but that's another story). I got dressed up in my best clothes and went downtown with Dad.

I told the bank manager about the coin set I wanted to buy, how I had $100 saved up and needed an additional $200. I told him I had a steady income from my job doing newspaper collections and could afford to pay back $10 a month. We talked about how I managed my money, how I had saved the $100 and why it was important to me to buy the coin set. Out came the forms, which I signed (and Dad countersigned), and presto! My bank account had $300 in it and I was able to buy the coin set.

I have a crystal-clear memory of walking back to the car with Dad and him saying to me, 'Now, David, there is one important thing you need to remember. What you borrow, you must pay back.' Those words have stuck with me throughout my life.

Over the next two years, I made sure to put at least $10 into the bank account every month to repay the loan. I didn't know it at the time, but when I turned sixteen, I had a good credit rating.

I'll never forget the words my dad spoke as we left the bank back in 1976: 'What you borrow, you must pay back.' If you don't, or if you breach certain terms of the loan agreement, this has serious negative implications.

For a start, the company's credit rating will be impaired, making it harder to borrow money in future. With the widespread sharing of credit information, this poor credit rating will be known to all institutional lenders, suppliers and anyone who has access to credit agency reports.

Furthermore, loan agreements typically have default provisions which, among other things, mean the lender can charge a higher rate of interest while the loan is in default. Instead of, say, an 8% interest rate on the loan, the default rate might be 20%. It can quickly get *very* expensive.

In addition to this, the lender has the right to exercise their security charges. This means, for example, they can take over the accounts receivable and collect them, starving the company of incoming cash. The lender can seize assets and sell them in the open market. They can make changes to the management of the company, including firing members of the executive team – even the founders.

In extreme cases, the lender can wipe out the shareholders and take control of the equity. In one of the acquisitions I completed, the company was backed by a private equity house which had put in a sizeable loan. When the company defaulted, it triggered a clause which meant the private equity house as debt holder ended up owning 99.99% of the fully diluted equity in the business. Everyone else's share – including that of the founders, investors and staff who had options – was wiped out.

Debt can be an incredibly powerful tool in your growth strategy; just be sure you do not default on the conditions of the loan. In addition to the repayment of principal and interest when it is due, you must also fully understand and comply with the reporting requirements and covenants which are part of the facility agreement.

We'll take a look at both of those.

Reporting requirements and covenants

Reporting requirements are linked to providing your lender with regular financial information, typically in the form of monthly or quarterly management accounts, as well as the full financial statements after the end of each year. The lender may require you to have the financial statements audited, so watch out for that.

Generally, the lender will want to receive copies of management accounts within ten days of the end of each month or quarter, so be sure your finance team has the ability to produce them within the required timeframe. Being late can trigger default provisions. Annual financial statements usually need to be submitted within ninety days of year-end.

Depending on the nature of the business, there may be other metrics the lender requires. These will be set out in the facility agreement. There will also be things like reporting if you are ever threatened or served with litigation. Be aware of these and comply with them.

Let's move on to covenants, which is lending-agreement speak for promises. Covenants fall into two types: positive and negative. Positive covenants are things you must do, for example provide audited financial statements within ninety days of year-end, maintain agreed levels of insurance on the business and key people within it, or retain membership in whatever trade or professional association you may be a member of.

Negative covenants are things you must not do – for example, certain financial ratios, like total debt on the balance sheet must not exceed three times earnings before interest, taxes, depreciation and amortisation (EBITDA); debt servicing costs (the sum of all interest and principal payments over the next twelve months) must not be more than EBITDA; or the company may not pay any dividends or take on any other debt funding; as well as non-financial covenants like not shutting down any operations or trade of the business. These can be complex and I urge you to take professional advice whenever you enter into a loan agreement. Be aware of the covenants and comply with them.

Let's have a brief look at PGs. While some of the FinTech companies which are springing up do make it easier and faster to borrow money than banks, they want a PG. If you refuse, you won't get funding from them.

The great thing about having a limited company is it limits the liability to the legal entity. With relatively few exceptions, the shareholders of a limited company are protected from having to pay in any additional resources, even if the company falls on hard times. This is sometimes referred to as the corporate veil. Granting a PG completely bypasses that, because the guarantor is putting their own assets (home, pension, savings, car, etc) on the line as part of the security for the debt. Lenders always want it if they can get it. If you can in any way avoid granting a PG, please do.

A final word of advice if you ever take on debt finance. If there are signs that something may be about to go wrong in the business, keep your lender informed. Do not try to hide it; be proactive and tell them. Many responsible lenders will work hard with their borrowers to ensure the loan stays current.

For example, during the financial crash in 2008–09, I was able to negotiate a waiver of covenants on more than $10 million of debt funding which would otherwise have been breached and put the facility into default. I was able to secure a waiver from the lender because I had maintained an open and professional relationship with them and kept them fully informed as to what was happening in the business.

ABC TAKES ON DEBT FUNDING

The business was growing. Annabel's idea had been well received in the consumer market and sales were booming. Briony had developed the hardware and software into a funky little device which did exactly what it was meant to do, and she was showing a real flair for design as well as making kit that worked.

Customers loved the product. Operationally, things were challenging and the three co-founders were constantly struggling to keep up with demand. One day, Charlotte announced she had just landed a large corporate customer that wanted to roll out the device to its workforce worldwide. With this one client, ABC was going to sell more units than it had sold in the past twelve months. Something had to change for the co-founders to service this new business and keep growing the company.

The three co-founders sat down to brainstorm possible solutions. As ever when they needed to tap into their deeper selves and get the creative juices flowing, Charlotte put on a fusion jazz playlist in the conference room at their offices. After a couple of hours, they invited the other members of the executive team – the heads of operations and finance – to talk through the ideas they had come up with. They quickly reached agreement that the best solution would be to bring production in-house.

Up to that point, they had outsourced production to a large contract manufacturer. ABC wasn't big enough to be important to the manufacturer and as a result, the business wasn't getting its deliveries on a timely basis. This had been the business's biggest headache.

Bringing production in-house meant acquiring machinery and equipment, taking on additional premises and hiring a new team to make the device. Briony agreed to work on this with the heads of operations and finance, and within a week, they came back together with the other two co-founders to outline a plan of how to make it happen. They needed to raise more than ABC's sales revenue from the past twelve months to finance the plan, but the head of finance could clearly show that, with the new corporate contract in place, ABC Limited would generate enough positive cash flow to pay back the funding over the next three years. In addition, this would give them sufficient capacity to continue growing the consumer side and take on another corporate customer of the same size.

Given the biggest element of expenditure would be machinery and equipment to make the device, the head of finance recommended to the co-founders that debt would be the best way to finance this growth. They had a clear plan showing the company had the cash flow to service the debt, thanks to this new contract, and there were physical assets which the lenders could place a charge on, which gave added security.

Annabel, Briony and Charlotte put in a call to the relationship manager at their bank, who referred them on to the bank's asset finance division. This was a specialist team, focused on lending to businesses that were purchasing physical equipment. It took a couple of months to get everything in place, with the bank scrutinising ABC's plans in great detail, meeting with the manufacturer of the equipment and going through the technical specifications with a fine-tooth comb, and of course getting all the legal documents in place for the lending facility, including negotiating covenants, security and other reporting requirements.

After hard negotiations, the bank accepted that, with security over the new equipment and the business as a whole, it would not require PGs from Annabel, Briony and Charlotte. It was the hardest part of the negotiation and the three founders had to remain closely aligned throughout to win that concession from the bank.

The founders signed the facility agreement, the money arrived in their account and they executed their plans to bring production in-house.

Chapter wrap

What you borrow, you must pay back.

Debt can be a useful source of funding for businesses at every stage, and it is vital for those who need capital, but choose not to sell equity. Particularly for businesses with physical assets and predictable cash flow, significant sums of debt funding are available. Debt does not dilute the owners' equity stakes, but it comes with cash flow and compliance challenges.

6

From Bootstrapping To Angel Investors

From here on, we will be looking at equity funding. When you raise money by selling equity (shares in the limited company), the investor has an ownership stake in the business. You don't have to pay them back, but if the company pays dividends, the investors are entitled to their fair share. If you sell the business, they will be entitled to their percentage stake in the price you sell for.

Bootstrapping

This is how most businesses start out. You get an idea for a product or service the market needs. You create it and sell it. Until the first money comes in from a paying customer, it's down to you to finance both your business and your life.

Many founders choose not to take any money out of the business, instead relying on their savings or their partner, friends and family to keep them going. It's a tried-and-tested route and many consider it to be the honourable way to get started. Indeed, I know from my discussions that early-stage investors and successful entrepreneurs often see it as a rite of passage.

I agree with them. Up to a point.

It is crucially important in the early days of a business to prove you have the hustle and your idea about a market need can be shown in the only arena that counts: the market itself. Until you have sold your product or service to someone independent from your family and circle of friends, it's just an idea. Making the first truly independent sale is the crucible.

From that point, you have market proof. Then the challenge is to get out there and do it again and again, and again. Once you have done this, you know you're really on to something. It's a great feeling, but it's also a trap, because bootstrapped businesses have limited funds to grow.

CHALLENGING CONVENTIONAL THINKING

The pace of change in today's world is so fast, you need to think differently if you want to get ahead. It's the only way.

You can, of course, choose not to change. You can slog it out in your industry, fighting battles with the same competitors, undercutting them to win the next job, but it's a race to the bottom. It's sad, really. In my years in business, I've come across so many entrepreneurs who started out with a dream, and then reality bit them. Hard. I've seen founders who had great vision, but ten years on, their business still hasn't broken through seven-figures in sales. They barely take a holiday, and when they do, they're always on the phone or the laptop back to the office. It takes a huge toll on their family. Some are still struggling to get by on average earnings. Their dream is dead and they feel trapped.

Instead of growing, they cut back to save money. 'Let's spend less on marketing. We don't need to update our website, it's only five years old. It's hard to find skilled workers and they're so expensive. Let's get cheap ones instead.' It works, for a while, but it makes it impossible to grow a business.

It's a mindset thing. If all you think about is cutting back and saving money, you'll never break out of that rut. It's pervasive. Your staff and culture soon reflect it.

Everything we experience in life is dependent upon our thinking in the moment. The world outside us is not responsible for our experience and how we feel about it; the world outside us merely gives us input through our five senses. Only we are able to decide how we feel and our way of thinking affects that. Most times, it doesn't seem that way, but it really is how it works.

This isn't just some new-age hippy thing. There's a wonderful quote from Henry Ford, perhaps the most successful entrepreneur of his time, who said over 100 years ago, 'Whether you think you can, or you think you can't – you're right.'

Viktor Frankl was a Jewish prisoner of the Nazis in World War II. All his family were killed in concentration camps, but he survived and thrived (as much as one can under such inhumane conditions). Frankl discovered that, no matter what his captors did to him, he retained the final freedom: to choose how to react to what was happening to him. His thinking led to him being described as the freest man in those death camps.

What does all this mindset stuff have to do with entrepreneurship and growing your business? Everything, really. Changing your mindset allows you to change the rules of the game. It's about having an open mind and the willingness to challenge what many people perceive as conventional wisdom, or indeed common sense.

Friends and family

It's important for you to be open-minded to the potential of growing faster. The challenge is: growing fast is expensive. You need to hire more staff to win and deliver the business. You need to spend more on marketing. You need to upgrade your delivery infrastructure. Everything needs to grow and that kind of growth devours cash like nothing you've seen before.

If you want to grow slowly, keep on bootstrapping. If you want to grow fast, you need to raise some cash, and the first place you can turn for this is your friends and family.

Many people instinctively shy away from this. It might have been OK to borrow a few grand from your parents or your wealthy uncle to get you going, but reaching out to your wider family and your friends? That feels weird.

This is where your mindset needs to change. At this stage, you have an idea which has some traction and you need money to make it happen. Think of it as another business transaction. Think of it as an opportunity for you to share what you are doing with your community, with the people who know you and care about you. It's not like going cap in hand and asking for a handout or a favour or some charity.

If that mindset is holding you back, you need to go inside yourself and explore why. Get comfortable with the idea of raising money for your business. You aren't asking for a handout; you're offering something of value.

ABC RAISES ITS FIRST FUNDING

To get the business off the ground as a brand-new startup, the ABC co-founders knew they needed to spend some money. They also knew it would initially have to come from themselves until they were in a position to get some sales revenue going, and they agreed to each put $25K of cash into the company so they could get the first version of the product built.

Annabel had her redundancy money, so was able to use that. Briony didn't have that kind of money and neither did her parents, but her aunt and uncle ran a small business and Briony was able to convince them to back her. They loaned her $25K to put in her stake.

Charlotte had saved all the money she had made from drumming gigs over the last forty years and invested it in the stock market, so she had a nice little portfolio of stocks. She sold a couple of holdings and put in the cash. In effect, ABC's initial financing was part bootstrapping and part friends and family.

The co-founders agreed that in the early days, until they started generating revenue, they had to run lean. None of them took a salary for the first several months while they concentrated on getting the product-market fit right. They each worked from home and met in cafes when they needed to be face-to-face.

A big chunk of the initial funds went on a 3D printer for producing the prototype. Briony thought it would be OK to get a cheap one to start with, but Charlotte and Annabel had other ideas. After lengthy discussion, they convinced Briony it made sense to buy the 3D printer they would use for their initial production runs rather than going for a cheap one. That way, once they knew the prototype was right for production, they wouldn't then have to go out and find a printer capable of making the device; they'd already have it and could simply go from test runs into full-blown production.

The other big spend was on getting their IP protected. Annabel had learned about IP in her corporate job and knew it was critically important they get the right protection. After meeting with several IP lawyers and patent attorneys, the co-founders agreed getting a patent was the best route. The idea was unique and Briony was building both hardware and software, so it met the necessary tests.

By the time the first production units were coming out of the 3D printer, Annabel, Briony and Charlotte were proud to see the words 'patent pending' on the underside of the device. It had been a big investment up front, one they would in later years be thankful they had made.

During the time Annabel and Briony had been getting the device just right, Charlotte had been reactivating her network of contacts and developing several potential routes to market. She visited a number of retailers and distributors to tell them about the product. She also researched the direct-to-consumer market.

Everything came together nicely, and within a few months, ABC had secured its first sales. It was exciting for the co-founders to see some cash coming into the company, but also a little scary to see how quickly it needed to go out again. They soon realised that getting a business off the ground devours cash.

Crowdfunding

Crowdfunding enables companies to raise money from a large number of people – ie from 'the crowd'. Typically, investments on crowdfunding sites range from $10 to tens of thousands or more. Crowdfunding has changed the rules of the fundraising game; some sites offer debt, some equity. There are even sites where the business raising money can ask for donations or offer gifts in exchange for funding. Wherever in the world you are, you only need to google 'crowdfunding' to find a multitude of sites you can use to raise money.

Have a look on each site at other companies which have raised money. Learn what works and what doesn't by reviewing both companies which are doing well and those which aren't succeeding. Perhaps in the case of the latter, the business plan is not sound, the video needs work or the market for the product doesn't exist.

Crowdfunding sites have a serious vetting process, which includes testing your business plan and assessing whether there is, in fact, a market for your product. In the past, I have helped clients raise money with Crowdcube in the UK and have been told only one in three companies applying actually passes the vetting stage.

How does it work? It depends on the site. On Crowdcube, companies offer shares in exchange for money given by investors. Alternatively, sites like Kickstarter offer gifts in exchange for donations.

Provided it has a solid business plan and a clear vision, even the smallest startup can successfully raise money through crowdfunding. Perhaps you haven't made your product yet, but you are confident of the market. As long as you have clearly laid out your plan and the milestones you hope to achieve, crowdfunding can be for you.

CROWDFUNDING SUCCESS FOR FEMALE FOUNDERS IN AUSTRALIA

An article published in *The Chainsaw* in 2021 featuring the Australian crowdfunding site Birchal (www.birchal.com) reported that female founders raised on average 25% more funding than male-led businesses on its platform during 2020, with the largest raise being $2 million by the Aussie cult hot-sauce brand Bunsters.

The key to success in crowdfunding is an engaged community of fans and followers. These may be customers, suppliers or a wider community of people who support you and your business. In many cases, female founders have been more successful than their male counterparts in tapping into their fans and followers to secure funding.

Crowdfunding is still relatively new in Australia. A female ride-sharing company called Shebah, which raised $3 million – including $1 million from one investor – is still the largest crowdfunding raise in Australian history.

Matt Vitale, managing director of Birchal says equity crowdfunding is one of the few places to present a level playing field: 'To the extent that such bias exists, equity crowdfunding has the potential to neutralise it, by providing founders with an alternative source of capital. We think this is a really exciting trend, that could help to improve the representation of other minority groups among startup founders.'

Angel investors

For many entrepreneurs, angel investing is the next step up from bootstrapping or friends-and-family investment. The sums are greater, the investor involvement is higher and it is slightly trickier to access, but the payoff from a successful relationship with an angel investor can be huge.

Typically, angels operate in networks and several members will team up to make investments in qualifying companies, usually up to $500,000, but occasionally much more. Angel investors tend to be wealthy individuals who have a background in business and investment. Often, they are entrepreneurs themselves who have sold a business and want to invest their money in companies they perceive to have a good trajectory for growth. It's not just about the cash, though; angels will get involved in the strategic decisions of your company, lend their expertise and open their book of contacts to your business.

Chances are you've seen or at least heard about TV shows like *Dragons' Den* or *Shark Tank*. The people who sit back and listen to entrepreneurs pitching to them are angel investors, although in real life, you won't be pitching to people who have stacks of cash on the table in front of them. Make no mistake: angel investors have the money as the syndicates vet them before they are able to join, but the piles of cash are just for the TV cameras.

Unless you know someone who is an angel investor, you may be wondering, 'Who are these people and how do I make contact with them?' The first step is to ask people in your network if they know anyone suitable. Perhaps you have a friend who works in a law or accountancy firm. Those firms are often involved with business deals and your friend could make an introduction, either to the angel or to a more senior person in the firm who has dealings with angel investors.

A good place to start is with a Google search. This might point you to a trade body like the UK Business Angels Association (www.ukbaa.org.uk), the Angel Capital Association (www.angelcapitalassociation. org) which covers North America, Business Angels Europe (www.businessangelseurope.com) or something similar wherever you live. If you can't find anything locally, I would start with the World Business Angels Forum (www.wbaforum.org).

LinkedIn is another great place to find angel investors. You can search for people who have 'angel investor' in their profile description – a search I did just now came up with 68,000+ results, so you may need to narrow your search criteria a little. Read their profiles to understand if they are the right person for you to connect with, and if so, reach out and connect.

Attend angel investor events. You can often find them through the sites I've noted or search for them on meeting information sites like Meetup or Eventbrite. You can also do some deeper research. Look out for news in your industry or your local area about businesses which have recently been sold or have secured investment. Reach out and make contact with the owners.

Many angels operate through networks as opposed to on their own. Networks are formed of a group of angel investors and typically have one person who acts as the coordinator. This individual may or may not be an investor, but they are of critical importance as they are the gatekeeper to the network.

NIGEL JOINS ABC AS ANGEL INVESTOR

Annabel, Briony and Charlotte put together a business plan showing that, with an investment of $250,000, they would be able to garner significant market share and establish ABC as a leader in its sector. They knew what to spend the money on and what needed to happen to deliver a strong return.

Annabel knew a member of the World Business Angels Forum and she reached out to them. This contact suggested they start by researching a number of angel investor networks and making contact with the main coordinator of the ones which appeared most relevant to them.

After searching on Google, Annabel, Briony and Charlotte identified seven angel networks which might be a good fit with ABC and dug further into them. It was sometimes difficult to get all the information they needed as angel networks can be quite secretive, but in the end, they managed to identify the gatekeepers at four. They did more research on these four and, through LinkedIn, were able to identify contacts in their networks who could introduce them to two of the gatekeepers.

They approached all four network gatekeepers – two with an email introduction from mutual contacts and the other two cold – and were able to secure appointments with both introduced gatekeepers and one of the others. Following pre-qualifying calls with the three gatekeepers, Annabel, Briony and Charlotte were invited to pitch ABC's investment case to two networks.

Annabel, Briony and Charlotte spent the next few weeks rehearsing their pitch presentation and trying to anticipate the kinds of questions they might be asked. When the dates for their pitches arrived, they were ready. In one case, they found themselves pitching to eight people, and in the other, fifteen.

The pitches went well and they had interest from both networks. They were particularly attracted to one of them where a chap named Nigel had a background in technology and was experienced in the industry their product was targeted at. It looked like a match made in heaven – no wonder they are called angels.

The deal was negotiated between ABC and Nigel, who was representing the network. In the end, ABC secured the full $250,000, with Nigel investing $150,000 and two other members of the network putting in $50,000 each. Nigel was appointed as a director of the company to work closely with the three co-founders over the next two years as the business grew and developed.

It wasn't always smooth sailing. Development of the technology took nearly twice as long as anticipated, which put a serious burden on ABC's cash flow. Nigel remained supportive of the business, but for nearly six months, he turned up the heat on Annabel, Briony and Charlotte to get the situation under control.

Once things recovered and the business was back on track, Nigel agreed to open his little black book and make a number of introductions which would be hugely beneficial to ABC. By the end of the second year, the business was growing ahead of plan and the angels were pleased.

Chapter wrap

All the sources of funding we've looked at in this chapter are from individuals: the founders themselves for bootstrapping; friends and family to help through the bootstrapping phase; and crowdfunding, which has democratised access to investment in SME businesses. Sure, there are professional investors on the big crowdfunding sites, but a huge amount of the investment activity comes from individuals who want to support SME businesses. Perhaps none more so than angels – usually wealthy entrepreneurs who have successfully grown and sold their businesses, and can offer the benefit of their experience along with funds.

7
Institutional Investors

We now move into the arena of professionally managed money. With crowdfunding and angel investors, you are typically dealing with the person who is investing their own money, whereas with institutional investors – VC, private equity (PE), wealth management firms and family offices – the people investing the money are doing so on behalf of someone else. True, in many cases, the investors will also put some of their own money into a deal, but the vast majority of the money being invested belongs to someone else.

The money behind the investment may be from a pension fund, a university endowment fund or a wealthy individual or family being managed across generations. Because of this, the checks are tougher and the investor involvement is higher.

Venture capital

VC is incredibly competitive with many VC firms receiving thousands of proposals each year. For this reason, an introduction to the firm is extremely beneficial.

VC firms tend to specialise in a specific industry or sector of an industry. It may be they invest in FinTech, media or healthcare-related businesses, but their focus tends to be narrow and each will have an expert in the field. This person will be brought in to dissect and challenge your business plan, so it must be rock solid. Companies generally raise between $500,000 and $10 million using VC firms, so although the risk is high for both company and investor, the growth potential is tremendous.

I spoke recently with the managing partner of a mid-sized VC firm in London. He told me in the past twelve months, the firm has received more than 1,000 pitch decks and it has made sixteen investments. It's a *very* competitive environment, even without considering the uneven playing field female founders face.

With unsolicited or unintroduced plans, it's not uncommon for the most junior member of the firm to have a checklist and spend five to ten minutes (sometimes not even that long) skimming through each plan to assess whether it qualifies for investment. You must grab their attention in this time.

For this reason, it is a good idea to find someone you know to introduce you to a VC firm. Reach out to your friends or to a successful entrepreneur. Get to know lawyers and accountants as they are well connected. Go to pitching events, where you can watch and learn as well as network. Most of all, take time for initial research and clear targeting of the right VC firms for your business. This is critically important, especially if you don't have the contacts to make an introduction.

The VC firm will structure the investment deal in a way which protects its interests over everyone else's to ensure it gets its money first. The way it achieves this is via a combination of common stock and preference shares or debt, which we'll cover in detail later in this chapter.

If things go according to plan, VC can be incredibly useful. Depending on the VC firm you are with, if the business grows as predicted, it can be easy to raise even more money to grow further and faster. Serial entrepreneurs who have had success with one company can often go back and ask for more money to grow the company or invest in their newest venture once they have exited their previous one.

When things don't go according to plan, though, there is a darker side of the VC world. I have seen it. Make no mistake: a VC firm's number-one focus is to protect its investment and hopefully see a return. Venture capitalists will be supportive when a business hits the inevitable bumps in the road and will help the founders get through them, but if the problems are more serious than that, they can insist on major changes, including personnel changes, to get the business back on track. As one friend of mine describes it, 'They can be all over you like a rash.'

CHANGES AS ABC SECURES VC FUNDING

A few years after Nigel and his network invested in ABC, the business was growing well and the founding team decided to expand the company by targeting a new industry vertical showing great potential. Nigel was supportive of this move, but his angel network didn't have access to the $3 million which ABC required to make it work. Fortunately, Nigel had good contacts into a leading technology VC firm which had funded one of his early ventures and done well from the deal.

Nigel was able to secure a meeting with his friend Rebecca, one of the partners in that firm. This was hugely beneficial to ABC since none of the founders had any VC contacts.

Knowing VC firms are data hungry, Nigel was able to guide the founders in putting together a compelling presentation with the level of detail he knew Rebecca and her colleagues would want to see. They met at the VC firm's offices. Rebecca was there with another partner, three analysts and a person who was introduced as the VC firm's technology expert. Expert he was, with PhDs from both Cambridge and MIT. Every technology deal this VC firm considered at partner level had to be passed by him before it would make the investment.

It was a gruelling meeting with detailed questions coming from every conceivable angle, and at the end Rebecca said she would get back to ABC within a few days. The wait was agonising. The expert had given nothing away when the ABC representatives answered his questions. He was stone-faced and spoke in a soft monotone. The other members of the VC team had also been at pains to appear neutral throughout the meeting. Nigel tried to reassure them the pitch had gone well, but Annabel, Briony and Charlotte were anxious. They had never been subjected to that level of scrutiny or questioning before and had no idea whether it would be a yay or a nay.

Three days later, Rebecca rang with good news. The VC firm was interested in making the full $3 million investment, but she and her colleagues were challenging the valuation of ABC and wanted a bigger stake than they had been offered. After lengthy discussions between the founders, Nigel and his co-investors, they agreed to accept the indicative offer.

The next step was for the VC firm to conduct due diligence. Nigel had warned the founders that ABC would be carrying the cost and they had already set aside funds to cover it. Representatives from top law and accountancy firms showed up at ABC and crawled all over the books for two weeks. The technology expert spent several days going through ABC's code and plans for developing the product for the new industry vertical.

ABC passed the due diligence and the terms of investment were agreed. As part of the deal, the VC firm appointed an independent chairman of the board from its network of approved chairs and Rebecca also joined the board of ABC.

The business continued to grow successfully over the next several years. It was a real adjustment for the founders, though, because the company had to grow up quickly. Things became much more formal: there were monthly board meetings and the independent chairman was a stickler for ensuring the board operated properly, distributing comprehensive packs a week before each meeting which he expected everyone to read and digest so they could have meaningful discussions as a board. Early on, Briony made the mistake of not reading the pack before a board meeting and was unable to answer a number of key questions which came up in the discussions. Following the board meeting, Briony was invited to a private meeting with the chairman. She never made that mistake again.

Private equity

Like venture capitalists, PE firms will pool money from wealthy investors and manage it in a professional fund. Unlike venture capitalists, PE firms are risk averse and tend to invest in established businesses with a proven track record.

PE firms typically will not deal with early-stage companies. Unless you are a really established entrepreneur, it is unlikely they will be on your immediate investment horizon, but if you have had success with a VC firm and achieved solid growth, they may take on your business and help you expand into realms you hadn't ever imagined.

To successfully raise money with a PE firm, you will need to demonstrate that your business has good profits, several years' worth of audited financial statements and a solid management team. You will also need a high level of sales: anywhere upwards of $10 million a year. As well as this, you will need a connection into the PE house. They don't receive thousands of applications a year like some VC firms do, but PE firms are still incredibly hard to get into.

One of the other big differences is PE houses usually seek to have majority stakes in the companies they invest in. They are after scale and want to have control.

PE BACKING AND A NEW CEO FOR ABC

Six years later, ABC had grown into a substantial firm, and Nigel and his network partners decided they wanted to realise the considerable gains they had made from their investment. As angel investors, they liked the thrill of early-stage businesses.

Rebecca's VC firm had also seen a significant return on investment. As the fund it had invested from was nearing maturity, the firm was keen to sell its stake and return cash to its investors.

Annabel, Briony and Charlotte wanted to stay with ABC, but none of them wanted to be the chief executive of a company with sales revenues of $40 million and more than 100 staff. They wanted to find someone with the skills and experience to run the business now it had grown.

Rebecca and the chairman agreed to conduct a search for an experienced technology CEO who was interested in buying into an established business and taking it to the next level. After a few months, they found Jennifer who had an impressive track record and had recently exited from a deal with a software as a service business in a completely different industry sector. Jennifer and the PE house backing her sold the business to one of the global tech companies and both were flush with cash.

Due diligence was not dissimilar to what ABC experienced when the VC firm invested so everyone was well prepared for it, having lived under the strict adherence to governance rules the chairman had insisted upon. They agreed a deal whereby Jennifer came in as the new CEO of ABC and bought a 7% stake in the company. Annabel, Briony and Charlotte held 14% each, and the PE house acquired the remaining 51% from the angels and Rebecca's VC firm.

Rebecca, Nigel and the former chairman resigned from the board. A new independent chairperson was appointed, along with a new CFO whom the PE house had worked with before. Two of the partners from the PE house joined the board as well.

Things went smoothly for a couple of years, until the next economic downturn and a global recession which lasted more than a year. Two of ABC's large customers went bust and many more had to rein in their expenditure. ABC's revenues were off nearly 20% compared to plan and the board acted swiftly to implement a serious cost-cutting programme.

Jennifer was decisive and put forward a plan to cut costs by 30% to ensure ABC could survive the economic downturn. This was a new experience for Annabel, Briony and Charlotte. Not since the first dip after Nigel joined the business had they faced such a challenge, and certainly not at this scale. It was hard. They had to make some difficult decisions and asked the staff to reduce their salaries rather than letting go employees, some of whom had been with them from the beginning. They knew it was right for ABC, but it was the hardest thing the three founders had had to do.

The downturn brought opportunities as well. Several competitors were struggling, having not reacted as quickly as ABC to the changing climate. The PE house had deep pockets and, after some discussions, the executive team decided to put forward an acquisition strategy to the board. Over the next twelve months, ABC raised more money from the PE house and bought three of its largest competitors, becoming the unquestioned number-one player in several vertical markets.

Family offices

The final area of institutional investors covers family offices and wealth management firms. Like the archetypal Swiss private banker, these are specialist investment firms that look after the portfolios of high and ultra-high net-worth people, and they are tasked with preserving and growing capital so it can pass from one generation to the next.

In many ways, these investment firms operate much like VC and PE firms. There are typically professional fund-management staff at the face of the firm and it is their job to look after their clients' money. Where these firms can differ – and this is especially true with family offices – is if you are able to connect with members of the family, who tend to be entrepreneurial. Then the discussion can often be more like when you are working with an angel investor. They get the thrill and the buzz of creating a new business and scaling it up in a way the professional investors have been trained not to react to.

It is often difficult to gain access to the family members, but if you do manage to do so, you can adapt your approach accordingly as typically you'll be dealing with another entrepreneur.

Structures in institutional deals

In most cases, when you are raising equity capital, you'll do it by issuing common or ordinary shares in the company; the terms may differ based on where you are, but these are the normal shares which give the owner a stake in the business. When you raise money through crowdfunding, angel investors and public markets, you'll typically be issuing ordinary shares. When you're raising from VC or PE firms, in the majority of cases, they will add in funding through debt or preference shares.

Let's use an example to illustrate this. Let's say you're doing a $10 million raise to scale the company or acquire a competitor. In cases like this, you will often form a new company as the fundraising vehicle. The company will issue a small amount of ordinary shares to you, your team and the PE house. Let's say the split is 55% to you, 5% to your team and 40% to the PE house. The shares will be issued for, say, $1, so on day one, there is $100 of share capital.

Next, the company will issue preference shares to the PE house. These shares might or might not have voting rights, but what they will have is a guaranteed 'dividend' which accrues to the holders of the preference shares. Let's say the company issues $10 million of preference shares and they include a cumulative 'dividend' of 10% per annum. This means every year, the holders of these shares accrue $1 million worth of 'dividend'.

I use 'dividend' in quotation marks because under international accounting standards, dividends on preference shares are accounted for like interest expense. If the dividends are cumulative, they happen every year and must be accounted for even if they are not paid out. This serves two purposes:

- It ensures the preference shareholders get a guaranteed return on their investment.

- It often wipes out any profit in the business because the $1 million dividend is accounted for like interest expense, so it reduces the company's profits.

The new company now has $10,000,100 in cash on its balance sheet, this being the $100 paid in for ordinary shares and the $10 million for preference shares. It then buys the shares in your original company. Now you and your management team, together with the PE house, own the business.

Let's fast forward five years and look at three possible outcomes:

1. Things have gone well and you sell the company to a trade buyer for $22 million.

2. Things have gone OK and you sell the company for $16 million.

3. Things haven't gone well and you sell the company for $12 million. It's still a gain on the original $10 million, but as you'll see, it's not a great outcome for you and your team.

What happens is the trade buyer acquires the shares and typically the fundraising vehicle will be wound up, but it's important to understand the way the money gets paid out.

Let's start with outcome 1. You've sold the business to a trade buyer for $22 million, so everybody wins. Here's how the cash gets paid out:

- The first $5 million goes to the holders of the preference shares, this amount being the cumulative $1 million dividend every year for five years. For the sake of illustration, I've ignored any impact of compound interest over the years of the dividends not being paid out. This would increase the amount paid here.

- The next $10 million also goes to the holders of the preference shares, this amount being the capital they paid in for the shares. This gets paid in preference to all other shareholders, hence the name.

- The remaining $7 million goes to the holders of the ordinary shares. Assuming there has been no change to the original allocations, you would get 55% or $3.85 million, your management team would get 5% or $350,000 and the PE firm would get the remaining $2.8 million.

In outcome 2, the cash proceeds of $16 million would be paid out like this:

- No change on the first $5 million, it's the cumulative dividend.

- No change on the next $10 million, it's the preference shares themselves.

That leaves $1 million remaining from the proceeds, and again it gets split based on the percentage of ordinary shares. You will get $550,000, your management team $50,000 and the PE house $400,000. Not so attractive, is it? Five years of hard work, and you and your team take just 600 grand.

Outcome 3 is even worse for you and your team. The cash proceeds of $12 million go like this:

- No change on the first $5 million, it's the cumulative dividend.

- The holders of the preference shares will get the remaining $7 million in settlement for their shares. It's a loss of $3 million compared with what they put in, but at least they get back something.

- The holders of ordinary shares get nothing.

If you'd put debt into the business instead of preference shares, it would be broadly the same outcome. The lender would have secured the debt over the trade and assets of the company, so the debt would be paid off ahead of everything else. There is an order to these things when a company is being wound up: secured creditors are at the front of the queue, followed by unsecured creditors, followed by preference shareholders. Only when everyone else has been paid in full does whatever is left go to the holders of ordinary shares.

Some people might say it's not fair, but it's the reality of how these deals work. The upside is great for everybody, but the impact of the downside can be serious and the management team can end up with nothing.

Chapter wrap

Institutional deals represent the next level up in raising funding for your business. This is where the amounts get serious, and the complexity of the deal structure and documentation of the agreements increases significantly.

In this chapter, we have explored VC, PE and family office funding, as well as setting out at a high level how these deals are structured and the pitfalls you as the founder need to be aware of before you go down the road of taking on institutional funding.

8

Ensuring You Raise Funding Successfully

Now you know what type of funding is right for you and your business, it's time to turn to the how. In this chapter, I set out the key steps to follow to secure the funding you need to grow your business. I'm not saying it's going to be easy. It isn't. It's so difficult and time consuming, fundraising can become a full-time job on top of your day job. This chapter will help you get through it.

Let me share a little context. Over the course of 2021, there was a huge increase in the volume of money invested into VC firms for deployment into promising startups. There was literally a wall of money out there. The problem is, there was also a huge increase in the number of startups seeking funding, as shown by my conversation with the managing partner of a London

VC firm that had received over 1,000 applications in a year from companies looking for funding and made just sixteen investments. That means just 1.6% of approaches resulted in funding. Discussions with a partner in a Silicon Valley firm were broadly similar.

Follow the steps set out in this chapter to maximise your chances of being in that 1.6% and securing funding.

Have your fundraising assets ready

Before you start on the fundraising journey, it is critical to have your fundraising assets ready. I'm not referring to the assets on your balance sheet; rather, it's the documentation and printed materials you will share with potential investors as the conversation develops.

Before approaching any investor, you want to have at least your pitch deck, financial projections and business plan ready in a data room or secure cloud drive which you can access easily. We'll look at each of those in turn.

The pitch deck is typically ten to fifteen slides, rarely more. You want to have one key theme on each slide and don't overload the slides with too much text. You want enough to capture the reader's attention and have them wanting more.

The typical decks my team prepares for clients have these twelve slides:

Cover slide – keep it simple. Just include the name of the company and say it's a fundraising pitch deck. Use an attractive image.

Elevator pitch – in one or two sentences you can say out loud in thirty seconds or fewer, express the gist of your business. Capture the investor's attention.

Team – I like to put this right up front, especially for businesses at a relatively early stage. More than anything else, investors want to know the people they are backing. Who are the key players? Have they done something like this before? What education or qualifications do they have?

Problem – explain your target customer's problem. Set it out clearly and concisely. Make clear how their problem is harming them or their business.

Solution – show how your business solves the customer's problem. You don't need to go into too much detail; just make it clear that for each problem on the previous slide, you have a solution.

Traction – this is all about how the market is reacting to what you offer. Have you made any sales yet? If so, state how much the business made and from how many customers. Have you signed any distribution or partnership agreements? Are you in advanced stages of discussion with any other customers?

Target market – just how big is your market? Investors want to see the potential for 100× returns, so you need to show a big market. This is usually set out in three measures: TAM = total addressable market, ie the entire potential market in the whole world; SAM = serviceable addressable market, ie the element of TAM you could reasonably go after, based on your product or service and geographic reach; SOM = serviceable obtainable market, ie the share of SAM your business would reasonably be able to capture.

Competition – who else is out there doing what you do? Many entrepreneurs believe what they are doing is unique. Investors do not like that approach. If nobody else is doing it, why should they back you? They perceive a higher risk if there is not a market out there. You need to think hard about this one.

Financials – keep this simple and graphical. You want to set out revenue, expenses and EBITDA projections over a five-year forecast period. Don't be conservative. You need to grab the investor's attention with the possibility of a big financial return.

Investment ask and exit plans – be clear how much you are looking for and what your exit strategy is. There is an ongoing debate about whether to indicate your valuation by stating the percentage of the company on offer or remain silent on this point. The trend is moving towards being open, so you might say, 'We are raising $3 million in return for a 30% stake in the company.' For the exit, again be specific. If it's a trade sale, who might you be selling to? Over what time horizon? At what exit valuation? Let the investor know your plans.

Use of funds – what are you going to be spending the money on? Your financial projections will help you here as the investor can see where the money is being spent. They will absolutely want to know what you plan to do with the money.

Thank you and contacts page – thank the investor for their time and set out how they can get in touch with you. Be sure to include your direct email, mobile phone number and company website address.

That's it. Twelve slides. You can add up to three more if you need to go further in explaining your tech or some other unique aspect of your business, but don't overdo it.

Financial projections should include any historical financial statements (if you have them) and a five-year forward projection. Work with your finance team to make sure the numbers are professionally produced and make sense. I've seen far too many business founders fall at this hurdle because the numbers don't stack up. If you don't have a qualified finance person in your team, now is the time to get one. Once you have investors on board, the demands on your team to produce regular in-depth financial reporting are going to grow.

In terms of the projections, you will need to produce numbers looking forward for a five-year period, including income statement, balance sheet and cash flow, on a month-by-month basis. Be sure to set out your key assumptions on revenue, market share and all areas of expense, so the financial plan can be updated as your assumptions and the reality of the market drive your decision making for the business.

Above all, when you're producing your numbers, don't be conservative. If you're going for external funding, you need to be telling a growth story, which means your revenues and expenditures will be growing. Growth is expensive and it eats cash. Investors know that. Build the financial plan to support the growth story you are telling.

Finally, there is the full business plan. This is a big written document – often thirty to fifty pages long – which sets out the detailed plan of what you aim to achieve and how you'll do it. Everything in your pitch deck and your financial model will be explained in the business plan.

When you have these three assets ready, you can start looking for investors, but the work on your assets doesn't stop there. You will need to pull together any other key documents into a data room, a secure Google drive or something similar, which you can share with investors when you get to the due diligence stage.

Researching and approaching investors

Now comes the hard work, the bit which is really time consuming. It's also the bit which is critically important to determining the success of your fundraising efforts. You may be wondering where to start. Who are these people and how do you find them?

Thankfully, it's not too difficult to find out who they are. Just google 'venture capitalists near me' or 'angel investors near me' and you'll get a few names. If you want to go a little more in depth, you could check out sites like www.angel.co or www.crunchbase.com where you can register and search their databases. Both sites offer free and paid-for access, and if you're serious about raising money, the few hundred dollars they charge for the paid access is worth it.

Another source which is focused more towards professional investors is www.pitchbook.com. Its subscription is rather more out of reach – in the tens of thousands of dollars – but you can register on its site and get access to lots of free resources, including industry reports which highlight key investors. It's well worth registering for a free account on all three.

The next step is to develop a longlist of potential investors from whatever sources you have used and drill into each of them. Go to their websites and see what they have to say. Some are secretive and only have a landing page with little else. Others go to great lengths to share with you their investment philosophy and even list the companies they have already invested in.

From the longlist, you want to develop a shortlist of thirty to fifty investors who are a good match with your business. Please do not follow the 'spray and pray' approach and simply spam everyone on your longlist. It won't work, and it could really annoy a potential investor who might otherwise have considered investing in your business.

In many cases, you will find investors are hard to get in touch with. This is where your additional work in the research phase will pay off. Check out the companies the investors show on their site. Maybe someone you know is in there. Look at those companies and identify parallels with yours. Reach out to the founders and connect with them using LinkedIn and other tools to expand your network. Ask them about their experience with the investor. Develop a relationship with these people, so ultimately you can ask them to introduce you to their investor contact. Studies continue to show a warm introduction is the best shot you'll have at getting a meeting which could lead to securing investment.

The other thing you'll find is many investors won't bother to get back to you. Some may have a comment on their site to the effect of: 'If we haven't replied within four weeks, you can assume your business is not a fit for us.' Others simply do not reply and leave the founders hanging on. Personally, I think this is both rude and lazy on the part of the institutional investors.

You need to understand the rules of the game before you play, and the rules apply to every type of fundraising except friends and family. Rule #1: put in the work at the research stage so your approach is intelligent and applicable to what your potential investor is seeking, and ideally get an introduction from someone they know. That gives you the best chance of securing a meeting, which is when you'll get your first chance to pitch. The other rules pale in comparison.

Pitching

Pitching is a process, a series of events rather than a single one. Wherever you are in the process, the goal of the pitch is to get to the next stage, just like advancing to the next level in your favourite game. It's important to understand this so you structure and deliver your pitch accordingly.

Many entrepreneurs ask me how much information they should share in the first pitch meeting. I always tell them to stick to the content of their first slide deck, which the investor will have received. Tell the story. The goal of the first meeting is to establish fit. If it's there, you may get a second meeting. If it's not, you don't want a second meeting.

At the first meeting, the investor has a few questions in mind:

- Do I like this person / these people?

- Do I understand the business?

- Does it have potential to scale?

- Can I add value beyond money?

Stick with what's in your deck and answer those questions. If both sides agree, then get ready for the next stage of the pitching process. Ask what the potential investor would like to delve into more. Be ready to give them more details and more answers.

Negotiating the deal

I could write a whole book about negotiating the deal. Maybe I should because space won't allow for it in this one.

Much like pitching is a process, so is negotiation, and there are three really important stages you will go through, plus due diligence. They happen in this order:

A verbal offer is made. This often comes at the end of a pitch meeting, when an investor will say something like, 'Yes, we will invest. We will put in $X and we want Y% of the equity.' Hurrah, you've got an offer. Fantastic news, but the deal is far from done at this stage.

The investor sends you a term sheet. This is a written document which sets out the key terms of the deal the investor is offering. At this point, you *must* engage lawyers to support you in the transaction, because these documents can be complex and you need to fully understand the terms on offer. Failure to do so could be catastrophic to your future success in this transaction.

Once you have signed the term sheet, **the due diligence process commences.** This is where the investor and their advisors (particularly lawyers and accountants) come into your business and crawl all over it. You need to be ready for this stage before it starts. The terms of the deal can be changed significantly, depending on what arises from the due diligence process. In some cases, the deal can even fall over.

The investor sends the investment agreement, which will often include a shareholders' agreement. This is the legally binding document which will set out all the terms of the deal, and once this is signed, the money will land in the bank. Again, you *must* engage lawyers to support you.

After the deal is done

In 1942, Winston Churchill said, 'This is not the end. It is not even the beginning of the end. But it is, perhaps, the end of the beginning.'

It's the same in the investment game. You've just entered a relationship which will likely last for at least five years. Maybe fewer, but equally, maybe more. There will be big changes to the way you and your business operate. There will be more formal governance, regular board reports and meetings, and shareholder meetings. It's a long-term relationship which can get very close and be very challenging.

You and your investor may one day be friends, but in business, they are not your friend. They represent their or their clients' money, and their job is to protect that money so one day they get it back, hopefully with a return. Keep the relationship on that level. Respect each other for the value you bring and be willing to listen.

I've met one or two entrepreneurs who didn't respect their investors and it's not a positive thing. For whatever reason, the relationship has broken down. Should you find yourself in this situation, in my experience, it's best to get out with the least damage possible to both parties.

These are the warnings. There are also many cases where things go well. The relationship builds, the company grows and perhaps the investor puts in more money to grow it further and more quickly.

Chapter wrap

This is the final stretch of the fundraising process. By following the steps set out in this chapter, you will maximise your chances of successfully raising funding.

Fundraising can be a full-time job on top of the day job. It can be physically, mentally and emotionally draining. Be sure to call on your team for help in this stage.

PART THREE
MAKING FUNDRAISING FAIR

Society evolves and develops. It usually takes a long time, but as people pick up the baton and drive change, it happens. When considering what needs to happen to make fundraising fair, we must look more widely at gender equality. In the words of former UN Secretary General Kofi Annan:

'Gender equality is more than a goal in itself. It is a precondition for meeting the challenge of reducing poverty, promoting sustainable development and building good governance.'

In this final section, we will look first at what needs to change in economic terms, then we will consider social and political change, and finally I set out for you what I am doing to help level the playing field.

9
Economic Change

Almost all the women I interviewed for this book have raised money across a range of industries and in amounts varying from a few hundred thousand to tens of millions of dollars. Over my career, I have raised more than $140 million in debt and equity funding. It is based on these interviews and personal experiences that I set out a vision of the economic change which needs to happen to make fundraising fair.

Is the fundraising industry broken?

There are record-breaking amounts of capital pouring into the VC and PE industries. There is an ever-growing number of angel investors and there are new crowdfunding sites appearing in many countries around the world. The fundraising industry is not broken per se; rather, the VC segment of the industry is – and to a lesser degree angel investors are – suffering from a myopic focus on trying to find the next unicorn.

Let's look a little more closely at the business side of running a VC firm. Once a VC firm has raised a fund of, say, $100 million, its job is then to invest that money. In addition, the firm has its own costs to cover – salaries, consultants, premises, research, etc – and it is common for it to charge a 2% annual fee to the fund, which in this case is $2 million. It will often charge fees to the investee companies as well, in return for services it provides by way of directors on the board, strategic input from experts and access to its wider community of contacts. For the purpose of this analysis, we'll ignore fees to the investee companies and just focus on the fund itself.

Over a five-year period, the annual fees to the fund add up to $10 million, which leaves $90 million to invest in companies. In our example, let's assume the VC firm invests in fifty different companies, so on average, the investment will be $1.8 million into each company. In practice, there will be a wider range, from $1 million up to $10 million and potentially more in one or two promising businesses.

Fast forward five years. In the portfolio of fifty companies, we might see these results:

- Ten companies have gone bust and the funds invested are lost.

- Thirty-five companies are still around, but they haven't really gone anywhere and the VC firm would be happy to find a buyer for them who will return some cash to the fund. If the firm cannot find a buyer, it might end up sitting on a 'zombie' investment: one which makes enough money to keep going, but not enough to reinvest in the business and grow it.

- Five of the companies are successful. Let's assume three of them return 3× on the investment (typically through a sale of the business), one of them returns 5× on the investment, and one of them becomes a unicorn, returning 100× on the investment. Based on the average investment of $1.8 million, that means three companies return $5.4 million ($1.8 million × 3) each or $16.2 million in total; one of them returns $9 million ($1.8 million × 5); and the unicorn returns $180 million. That's a total return to the fund of $205.2 million.

It's a numbers game which the venture capitalists and their investors understand. In our example, when the fund comes to the end of its life, the ten companies which went bust are gone; the thirty-five 'zombie' companies will be sold to the management or a turnaround specialist for a nominal sum; all the money comes from the five successful companies and the vast majority comes from the unicorn.

The final result from this example is:

- The VC firm's costs for the five-year period are covered from the initial fund.

- The investors get their $100 million back.

- There is an upside of $105.2 million which gets shared between the VC firm and the investors. It is not uncommon for the VC firm to get up to 20% of the upside, with 80% going to the investors.

On the other hand, in the absence of the unicorn, the return would have been $25.2 million. The VC firm's costs are still covered, but the investors receive just 15.2 cents on the dollar. That, dear reader, explains why the VC industry is so fixated on finding the next unicorn.

Bias directed against female founders

In the interviews I conducted, there were many stories from female founders of the overt bias and sometimes sexist comments they faced during the fundraising process. I shared some of these in Chapter 2. Here are a few more examples that were shared with me:

- 'I was attending a business networking event and experienced a number of patronising comments, the worst of which was, "You shouldn't come here looking for a husband."'

- 'I was attending a business event. After blanking me for most of the evening, a particular man came up to me when I was deep in conversation with someone he knew and said, "I want to know more about you. Tell me what your husband does."'

- 'I was attending an investor event and pitching with a male colleague. The investor completely ignored me. My male colleague had to turn towards me physically and say to the investor, "She can answer that better than me."'

- 'I was attending an angel investor event with a male business partner, whose company was using my software in its product. The partner told the angel he really ought to speak with me as my software was excellent and I was also raising. The angel wouldn't speak to me.'

- One founder said to me, 'I am over fifty and was asked by an investor if I really had the commitment and drive to build the business at my age.'

- 'I attended an event hosted by the VC arm of a major global corporate and was told by one of the investors, "The men who provide the funding want to see it invested in companies run by men like them."'

Bias is alive and well. We can change it over time, but for now, it's something female entrepreneurs must face. I share this so that, should you encounter it as a female founder, you'll know you're not alone.

What economic changes can we make?

Looking purely at economic issues and ways to improve access to funding for female founders, I have no doubt we need to address the bias. Over the long term, changes to the early education system, childcare and parental leave, and steps to improve safety and security will have a big impact. Significant funding will be needed and the funding needs to be sustainable.

In pure economic terms, I see three changes which will improve the situation:

1. Good financial education for everyone.

2. App-based micro finance.

3. A new kind of investment fund which is not fixated on finding the next unicorn.

Good financial education – there are many skills an entrepreneur should have. One which is overlooked or avoided by many is financial skills. This isn't about turning the world into a bunch of accountants. Rather, it is about ensuring everyone has sufficient knowledge of finance so finance will work in their life and in their business, and add value.

This education needs to be freely available to all, because it is not taught in most schools and is an invaluable life skill. The rollout would be funded through sponsorship from large corporate social responsibility budgets which are aligned with this mission.

App-based micro finance – this has the potential to truly change the world. There will be multiple regulatory hurdles to be jumped, but it will be worth it. Providing accessible micro finance across global mobile phone networks will enable as wide a reach as possible.

There continues to be great swathes of humanity who do not have access to banking facilities. Partnering with mobile telephone companies, this app could revolutionise these people's ability to conduct business transactions.

A new kind of investment fund – think Berkshire Hathaway but on a smaller scale. After all, Warren Buffett only does deals valued at $5 billion or more. Nonetheless, his philosophy is entirely understandable and he has proven over the long term to have outperformed all major stock-market indices. More importantly, he invests in businesses which have long-term potential and has often said his ideal investment horizon is forever. Compare that with the five- to seven-year focus of most angel and institutional investor funds.

A 2021 article by Seeking Alpha notes that, 'The cumulative returns are so massive that they are hard to get your head around – 2,810,526% for Berkshire over 55 years, 23,454% for the S&P 500.'

Put in other terms, Buffett has outperformed the S&P Index by 120 times. What investor would not want to see that kind of return?

Chapter wrap

In this chapter, we have looked at the fundraising industry and concluded that, while it is not broken, it still leaves a lot to be desired – especially for female entrepreneurs. We have revisited cognitive bias and seen more live examples. Finally, we looked at three changes which would have a huge impact on levelling the playing field.

10
Social And Political Change

In this chapter, we will look at perhaps the biggest gender-based social and political change in recent history, universal suffrage, to get a sense of the size and scale of the challenges ahead. We'll then look at the data from the most recent 'Global Gender Gap Report' published by the World Economic Forum. Finally, we'll take a look into the future to imagine a more equal world and identify what changes need to happen – socially and politically – to make fundraising fair.

The journey to universal suffrage

One of the most important societal changes in the 20th century was the granting of universal suffrage. It was a long, hard road to change, led in the United States of America by Susan B Anthony.

The movement in the USA began in the middle of the 19th century, when Anthony and her friend, Elizabeth Cady Stanton, founded the National Woman Suffrage Association. A few years later, in 1872, Anthony was arrested, tried and convicted for violating laws which only allowed men to vote. She was not allowed to speak until after the judge had returned his guilty verdict, when she delivered a strong rebuke to him:

> '...you have trampled underfoot every vital
> principle of our government. My natural
> rights, my civil rights, my political rights, my
> judicial rights, are all alike ignored.'

Anthony and Stanton were undeterred. In 1878, they were able to introduce into Congress a draft amendment to the US Constitution. It was another forty-two years before The Nineteenth Amendment to the US Constitution, which recognised the right of women to vote, was finally adopted and certified in 1920.

Across the Atlantic in the United Kingdom, Emmeline Pankhurst had been fighting the cause for women since the 1880s and she founded the Women's Social and Political Union (WSPU) in 1903. WSPU's motto was 'deeds, not words' and its members often took violent action, including smashing windows, arson and assaulting police officers.

In 1914, when the First World War began, Pankhurst called a halt to the militant activities of WSPU. She also wrote her autobiography, *My Own Story*, which opens with this statement:

'The militancy of men, through all the centuries, has drenched the world with blood, and for these deeds of horror and destruction men have been rewarded with monuments, with great songs and epics. The militancy of women has harmed no human life save the lives of those who fought the battle of righteousness. Time alone will reveal what reward will be allotted to the women.'

In 1918, the UK Parliament passed the Representation of the People Act, which gave the vote to all men aged twenty-one or more, and to women aged thirty or more who also owned land. This was a step in the right direction, although there was still a huge number of women who did not gain the vote. It took another ten years until the Equal Franchise Act 1928 was passed so that women in the UK had the same voting rights as men.

These important steps towards equality took place long before I was born, although there were many other countries around the world where universal suffrage took a long time to be introduced. In one case, I saw it first-hand. My wife and I moved to Switzerland in 1987. Women in Switzerland had only recently gained the right to vote in federal elections following a 1971 referendum. Perhaps more surprisingly, in the canton of Appenzell Innerrhoden, women still had no rights to vote on local or cantonal matters. They only gained that right after a decision of the Swiss Supreme Court in 1991. I remember being shocked about it.

It is astonishing that in the 21st century there are still a handful of countries which do not have universal suffrage. Afghanistan has had a tumultuous history, with equal rights for men and women implemented in a 1919 constitution which was thrown away ten years later. People regained the right to vote in 2004, although the current Taliban government is severely curtailing the rights of women since taking power again in 2021.

In Kuwait, men over the age of twenty-one have had the right to vote since 1962. Women did not gain the right until 2005. In Saudi Arabia, the right to vote in municipal elections was only granted to men in 2005 and to women in 2015.

We've come a long way in terms of universal suffrage. Let's use this as a beacon in the fight to make fundraising fair.

What about the gender gap?

Each year since 2006, the World Economic Forum has published the 'Global Gender Gap Report', which includes an index showing the gender gap by country. This isn't just about the gender pay gap; this index looks across four areas of society and compares the position of women versus men in 156 countries around the world. The four components to the index are economic participation and opportunity; educational attainment; health and survival; and political empowerment. The index score is the weighted average of the components.

The highest possible score on the index is 1, which represents complete equality between men and women. Scores below that reflect the amount of the gap. Based on the latest report, published in 2021, the global average index is 0.68. The report concluded that at the current rate of change, it would take 135.6 years to achieve parity worldwide.

If we look at each of the components at a global level, across all countries, health and survival achieved the highest score on 0.96, and educational attainment stood at 0.95 with thirty-seven countries now at parity. That's the good news. On the other hand, economic participation and opportunity was 0.58. The World Economic Forum concluded the size of this gap is caused by two trends:

'On one hand, the proportion of women among skilled professionals continues to increase, as does progress towards wage equality, albeit at a slower pace. On the other hand, overall income disparities are still only part-way towards being bridged and there is a persistent lack of women in leadership positions, with women representing just 27% of all manager positions.'

A long way behind is the fourth component, political empowerment, which scored just 0.22. The long, hard battles to win universal suffrage gave women equal rights to vote, but they still lag in terms of representing their people in government. The report found women represented just 26.1% of parliamentary seats and 22.6% of ministerial posts. More than half of countries had never had a female head of state.

Turning to individual results by country, just nine countries had an index score of more than 0.8. The top five were:

- Iceland – 0.892

- Finland – 0.861

- Norway – 0.849

- New Zealand – 0.840

- Sweden – 0.823

At the other end of the scale, two countries – Afghanistan and Yemen – had index scores below 0.5 and seven countries scored below 0.6. All were in the developing world.

We can learn a great deal about gender equality from the people of Scandinavia and New Zealand. Social systems in those countries are strong, and at the time of writing, four of the five countries listed have a female prime minister. The fifth country, Norway, had a female prime minister until late 2021.

A brave new world?

In looking to the future, I interviewed several female entrepreneurs and financiers to get their perspectives on what needs to change. I gave them the context of Emmeline Pankhurst, whose Votes for Women campaign in the United Kingdom took twenty-five years before all women had the same voting rights as men, and asked them to look twenty-five years into the future and consider what a fairer world for fundraising could look like. The interviews were eye-opening and I'm grateful to them for their valuable contributions.

The biggest learning for me from these interviews was the clear understanding that the uneven playing field of fundraising is merely a symptom of a wider malaise, and if we're to truly level the fundraising playing field, there are social, political and economic changes which must take place in the world first. When those underlying matters are addressed and resolved, there is a chance the playing field will level itself. There is still much to be done.

From the interviews, four main themes emerged around social and political change.

Nature versus nurture. In the nature versus nurture debate about children's development, unconscious bias is very much a nurture issue. It starts when children are young and it stays with them into adulthood. One of the interviewees mentioned a study commissioned by LEGO, which found that girls feel more confident about engaging in all types of play, but are still held back by gender stereotypes as they grow older.

In many cases, it is the parents who are driving the gender-biased behaviour:

'Parents from this study are almost five times as likely to encourage girls over boys to engage in dance (81% vs. 19%) and dress-up (83% vs. 17%) activities, and over three times [sic] as likely to do the same for cooking/baking (80% vs. 20%). Adversely, they are almost four times as likely to encourage boys over girls to engage in program games (80% vs. 20%) and sports (76% vs. 24%) and over twice as likely to do the same when it comes to coding toys (71% vs. 29%).'

Better access to childcare and freedom of choice for parents of any gender to remain at home with their children. Two of the interviewees have lived in Scandinavia for extended periods (recall the high scores of Scandinavian countries in the World Economic Forum report). Both referred to the fact that in many countries around the world, access to childcare is both difficult and expensive, and in some cases, the cost of childcare is greater than what the parent can earn by going back to work. As a result, one of the parents is forced to stay at home. Historically, in the vast majority of cases that parent was the mother, and it has impacted on her future career progression.

'Do Longer Maternity Leaves Hurt Women's Careers?', an article published in 2018 by *Harvard Business Review*, stated:

> 'Evidence from a variety of countries reveals that the longer new mothers are away from paid work, the less likely they are to be promoted, move into management, or receive a pay raise once their leave is over. They are also at greater risk of being fired or demoted.'

The article also found longer periods of parental leave led to the perception the parent was less committed to their job.

Ensuring safety and security considerations are no longer a gender-biased issue. The world will be a better place when both women and men can safely walk home at night. One of my interviewees, a single mum with two daughters, suggested boys and men often don't think about the risks of doing this and that it is a fundamental difference in how boys and girls are brought up. As the father of two (now adult) daughters, I hold this matter close to my heart. I remember telling my daughters to get a taxi home or phone me if they ever wanted to be picked up safely. Had my daughters been sons that would likely not have been the case.

To drive change in society, the people who run it must get behind the change and champion it. This is where political change steps in. The protagonists for change, like Susan B Anthony and Emmeline Pankhurst, had to lead the fight, but the real change came when they were able to secure the backing of people in government.

One of my interviewees was involved in driving change in the financial services industry in the United Kingdom. She had been pushing for change for an extended period of time, but it wasn't until the Governor of the Bank of England got behind her and championed her cause that real change happened.

Chapter wrap

In this chapter, we have reviewed the changes leading to universal suffrage, which now applies in all but a handful of countries around the world. We have looked at the 'Global Gender Gap Report' from the World Economic Forum and considered a number of key social and political issues which will play a huge role in helping to create a fairer society.

There is still a long way to go. Society evolves and develops, which usually takes a long time, but as people pick up the baton and drive change, it will happen.

11
What Am I Doing About It?

In the words of futurist Alan Kay: 'The best way to predict the future is to invent it.'

The future I am inventing starts with the creation of a new financial ecosystem, supporting every entrepreneur, regardless of their gender or any other characteristic. This ecosystem is based on the three key economic changes set out in Chapter 9: good financial education, app-based micro finance and a new kind of investment fund. The first two are long-term projects and will require a great deal of coordination on a national and, ultimately, global scale to implement. While not easy, the third change is already in progress. I am Co-Founder and CEO of Funding Focus Investment Trust plc, which is in process of seeking a

London Stock Exchange listing to support female and underrepresented entrepreneurs.

The goal is not to enter or disrupt the VC industry. Rather, it is to imagine a new financial services entity which takes the best aspects of the VC model and the Warren Buffett model and allocates funds to female founders and other underrepresented entrepreneurs. We have deliberately decided to seek a listing of the company on a major global stock exchange in order to ensure transparency and visibility. By having a public profile, we are in the strongest possible position not only to make the right investments but also to drive the social and political changes needed to level the uneven playing field.

It should be clear that my first priority is and will always be entrepreneurs. From the research I have done, I have crystal clarity that the quickest way to level the playing field is to start with the world of investment funding. That is where the change must start, and where the biggest opportunity lies. I must balance that priority with the needs of investors, and I am currently going through the launch process so am experiencing first-hand everything I have talked about in this book.

I'm not taking anything away from or competing directly with the VC industry. This is untapped potential which the VC industry is, for the most part, not looking at or even vaguely interested in. Let the venture capitalists chase the unicorns. There are plenty of good businesses which could become great businesses with the right funding and support.

This fund intends to focus on good businesses which are understandable, predictable and reliable (as much as that is possible). They will have some tech attached – any business without tech is on a downward path – but are not necessarily pure-play tech businesses. The fund will be focused on female-led businesses and will also invest in other underrepresented groups, rather than white male entrepreneurs who went to the same universities as the venture capitalists: Harvard, MIT, Stanford, Oxford, Cambridge and their counterparts in countries around the world.

At the time of writing, we are working through all the regulatory steps and the launch process.

Conclusion

The playing field is not level, although I can picture a fairer world than we live in today, a world where a single mum, a mixed-heritage couple and a disabled person have the same opportunity to secure funding and grow their business as a straight white man. We are each unique, and yet at the same time we are all made of the same raw life force. We can make a better world. A fairer world.

Thank you for starting this journey with me. I hope it's the beginning of a long and happy relationship. It is my sincere wish that you finish this book feeling uplifted. You face an uphill challenge and this book is your toolkit. It will help get you to your destination. You've read the facts and seen them come to life in the context of Annabel, Briony and Charlotte's business.

You've also explored stories of real people and their experience. Learn from them. Be inspired by them.

Entrepreneurs are the lifeblood of the global economy. We have the ability to course through the infrastructure which big business has created without being bogged down by it. We can nourish the world. Let us create a better and fairer world. Remember the $8.7 trillion opportunity? This is untapped economic potential which can be released and from which the world could hugely benefit.

Over to you. Only you can take the next step. The wonderful thing is you get to decide what the next step is. It's entirely your choice. My job has been to point you in a direction and to share experiences and stories you can absorb and apply in your world, whatever and wherever it is. My ask of you now is simply to take the next step.

In my fifty-nine years on this planet, I have experienced many times that the moment one commits and takes action, achievement becomes non-linear. You can certainly move step by step towards your destination – in fact it is all you need do – but along the journey, opportunities will present themselves. New people will appear. New contacts. New ideas. Be open to what this means. Achievement doesn't wholly depend on you. Please don't shoulder that burden. Your job is simple: hold your vision and take the next step.

If you need help or want more detailed instruction, please reach out to me. And please share your success stories with me. My social contacts are in the biography at the end of the book. You can also reach me via the website for my newest venture, Funding Focus Investment Trust plc: www.ffitplc.com

Being a man leading the fight for fairer funding is what I am supposed to be doing with my life. I will do everything I can to level the playing field.

I'll close with an extract from my favourite poem, 'The Road Not Taken' by Robert Frost:

Two roads diverged in a wood, and I—
I took the one less traveled by,
And that has made all the difference.

Bibliography

Abouzahr, K; Krentz, M; Harthorne, J; Brooks Taplett, F (2018) 'Why Women-owned Startups Are a Better Bet' (Boston Consulting Group) www.bcg.com/ publications/2018/why-women-owned-startups-are-better-bet

Annapurni, V (2020) 'Why Is the Funding Scenario Dismal for Women Entrepreneurs in India?' (*The Hindu Business Line*) www.thehindubusinessline.com/ companies/why-is-the-funding-scenario-dismal-for-women-entrepreneurs-in-india/article30997828.ece

Bennett, T (2019) 'Cover Story: Venture Capital Industry Is Allergic to All-Female Founded Businesses' (Which-50 Media) https://which-50.com/cover-story-venture-capital-industry-is-allergic-to-all-female-founded-businesses

British Business Bank (2019) 'UK VC & Female Founders' (British Business Bank) www.british-business-bank.co.uk/uk-vc-female-founders-report

Brodnick, E (2020) 'Diversity Beyond Gender' (Extend Ventures) www.extend.vc/diversity-beyond-gender

Buffett, WE; Munger, C (2000) 'Acquisition Criteria' (Berkshire Hathaway) www.berkshirehathaway.com/2000ar/acq.html

Campbell, R (2021) 'He Said He'd Invest $100K and Then Asked Me to Have Sex with Him' (Women's Agenda) https://womensagenda.com.au/latest/he-said-hed-invest-100k-and-then-asked-me-to-have-sex-with-him

CB Insights (2021) '$1B+ Market Map: The World's 936 Unicorn Companies in One Infographic' www.cbinsights.com/research/unicorn-startup-market-map

Church, J (2020) *Investable Entrepreneur: How to convince investors your business is the one to back* (Rethink Press)

Crotti, R; Kali Pal, K; Ratcheva, V; Zahidi, S (2021) 'Global Gender Gap Report' (World Economic Forum)

www.weforum.org/reports/global-gender-gap-report-2021

Derwin, J (2021) 'Female-led Startups Raised 25% More on Crowdfunding Platforms in 2020, Bucking the "Bias" of More Traditional Investors' (The Chainsaw) www.thechainsaw.com/female-startups-australia-crowdfunding-2021-1

Dooley, M (2019) *Infinite Possibilities: The art of living your dreams* (10th Anniversary Edition) (Atria Books/Beyond Words)

Dror, IE (2020) 'Cognitive and Human Factors in Expert Decision Making: Six fallacies and the eight sources of bias' (*Analytical Chemistry*, 92, pp 7,998–8,004)

Esposito, A (2019) 'More Funds Run by Daves Than Women' (*Morningstar*) www.morningstar.co.uk/uk/news/197122/more-funds-run-by-daves-than-women.aspx

Frost, R (1916) *Mountain Interval* (Quinn & Boden Co)

Gompers, P; Kovvali, S (2018) 'The Other Diversity Dividend' (*Harvard Business Review*, July–August 2018) https://hbr.org/2018/07/the-other-diversity-dividend

Gordon, AD 'Knowing Susan B Anthony: The stories we tell of a life', in Ridarsky, CL; Huth, MM (2012) *Susan B Anthony and the Struggle for Equal Rights* (University of Rochester Press)

Grady, C (2018) 'The Waves of Feminism, and Why People Keep Fighting Over Them, Explained' (Vox) www.vox.com/2018/3/20/16955588/feminism-waves-explained-first-second-third-fourth

Hideg, I; Krstic, A; Trau, R; Zarina, T (2018) 'Do Longer Maternity Leaves Hurt Women's Careers?' (*Harvard Business Review*) https://hbr.org/2018/09/do-longer-maternity-leaves-hurt-womens-careers

Higgins, ET (1998) 'Promotion and Prevention: Regulatory focus as a motivational principle' (*Advances in Experimental Social Psychology*, Vol 30, pp 1–46)

Hirschfeld, A; Gilde, J; Wöss, N (2020) 'Female Founders Monitor 2020' (German Startups Association) https://femalefoundersmonitor.de/en/female-founders-monitor-2020

HM Treasury (2019) 'Investing in Women Code' www.gov.uk/government/publications/investing-in-women-code

Horne, DB (2019) *Add Then Multiply: How small businesses can think like big businesses and achieve exponential growth* (Rethink Press)

Horne, DB (2020) 'The Fight for Fairer Funding' (TEDxPCL) www.ted.com/talks/david_horne_david_b_horne_the_fight_for_fairer_funding

Kanetkar, R (2021) '16 Black Female Founders in the UK Who Have Raised Funding' (Sifted) https://sifted.eu/articles/16-black-female-founders-uk

Kanze, D (2017) 'The Real Reason Female Entrepreneurs Get Less Funding' (TEDxPeachtree) www.ted.com/talks/dana_kanze_the_real_reason_female_entrepreneurs_get_less_funding

Kanze, D; Conley, MA; Okimoto, TG; Phillips, DJ; Merluzzi, J (2020) 'Evidence That Investors Penalize Female Founders for Lack of Industry Fit' (*Science Advances*, 6 (48)) www.science.org/doi/10.1126/sciadv.abd7664

Kay, A (1971) Speech at Xerox Palo Alto Research Center (Xerox PARC)

Lang, IH; Van Lee, R (2020) 'Institutional Investors Must Help Close the Race and Gender Gaps in Venture Capital' (*Harvard Business Review*) https://hbr.org/2020/08/institutional-investors-must-help-close-the-race-and-gender-gaps-in-venture-capital

LEGO Group (2021) 'Girls Are Ready to Overcome Gender Norms but Society Continues to Enforce Biases That Hamper Their Creative Potential' www.

lego.com/en-gb/aboutus/news/2021/september/lego-ready-for-girls-campaign

Pankhurst, E (1914) *My Own Story* (Hearst's International Library Co, London)

Pitchbook (2022) 'The European VC Female Founders Dashboard' (Pitchbook) https://pitchbook.com/news/articles/the-european-vc-female-founders-dashboard

Pitchbook (2022) 'The US VC Female Founders Dashboard' (Pitchbook) https://pitchbook.com/news/articles/the-vc-female-founders-dashboard

Priestley, D (2017) *24 Assets: Create a digital, scalable, valuable and fun business that will thrive in a fast changing world* (Rethink Press)

Priestley, D (2018) *Entrepreneur Revolution: How to develop your entrepreneurial mindset and start a business that works* (2nd edition) (John Wiley & Sons)

Rolfe, T (2021) 'Female Fund Managers Face 200-Year Wait to Catch Up to Men' (Nikkei Asia) https://asia.nikkei.com/Opinion/Female-fund-managers-face-200-year-wait-to-catch-up-to-men

Rose, A (2019) 'The Alison Rose Review of Female Entrepreneurship' (HM Treasury) www.gov.uk/

government/publications/the-alison-rose-review-of-female-entrepreneurship

Shaw, GB (1903) 'Man and Superman' [play]

Sloan, J (2021) 'Why Buffett's Berkshire Hathaway Is Still a Great Long-Term Holding' (Seeking Alpha) https://seekingalpha.com/article/4464166-berkshire-hathaway-stock-good-buy-long-term

Smith, SH (1968) 'A Case Study on Socio-Political Change' (*Phylon* 29 (4)) (Clark Atlanta University) www.jstor.org/stable/274023

Statista.com (2022) 'Global Gross Domestic Product (GDP) at Current Prices from 1985 to 2026' (Statista) www.statista.com/statistics/268750/global-gross-domestic-product-gdp

Statista.com (2022) 'Gross Domestic Product (GDP) in Current Prices of the United Kingdom (UK) from 1986 to 2026' (Statista) www.statista.com/statistics/263590/gross-domestic-product-gdp-of-the-united-kingdom

Teare, G (2021) 'Crunchbase Unicorn Board Leaps to Just Under 1,000 Companies, Reaches $3.4T in Value' (Crunchbase) https://news.crunchbase.com/news/crunchbase-unicorn-board-1000-companies

Teare, G (2021) 'Sole Female Founders Raised $1B Less in 2020 Despite Record Venture Funding Surge in the US' (Crunchbase) https://news.crunchbase.com/news/sole-female-founders-raised-1b-less-in-2020-despite-record-venture-funding-surge-in-the-us

Wickman, G; Paton, M (2014) *Get A Grip: How to get everything you want from your entrepreneurial business* (BenBella Books)

Women in VC (2020) 'The Untapped Potential of Women-led Funds' www.women-vc.com

Wood Brooks, A; Huang, L; Kearney, S; Murray, F (2014) 'Investors Prefer Entrepreneurial Ventures Pitched by Attractive Men' (Harvard Business School) www.hbs.edu/faculty/Pages/item.aspx?num=46891

Acknowledgements

There are many people who have contributed directly or indirectly to this book, and I'm grateful to all of them. If I've missed you in this list, I'm sorry.

Starting with my mum, Tricia Horne, who is 93 years old at the time of writing and who taught me about gender equality at a young age, long before it was a common thing to do. Thank you.

My wife Kate, whom I met when we were both seventeen. You are my rock, my life partner and my soulmate. Our daughters, Vicky and Madsie, who challenge me, support me, tease me and demonstrate every day what a joy it is to have kids, even when they are grown up. The three of you ensured that my mum's early lessons in gender equality stayed and evolved throughout my adult life. I love you more than you could ever imagine.

To 'Elizabeth', with whom I have unfortunately lost contact. Thank you for opening my eyes to the grave injustice that female founders face.

To Cindy Gallop, who challenged me to think much bigger than I had originally been thinking when I started writing this book. I have to admit, her comments initially did my head in, and it took me a couple of months of deep thinking before I was ready to crack on with the revised structure of the book. It was so worth it. Thank you also for writing the Foreword.

To the six brave souls who agreed to be test readers and gave so much useful and constructive feedback on the first draft of this book: Tammy Banks, Antonia Burridge, Angela Heylin LVO, OBE, Olivia James, Sophie Milliken and Maureen Sullivan. Your input has been invaluable, and you have my deepest thanks.

To the seven founders featured in Chapter 2: Fiona Lee, May Al-Karooni, Nan Williams, Dr Daniela Marino, Stacey Wallin, Lauren Lewis and Agnès Petit. Thank you for sharing your stories, experience and advice so freely.

To Drs Itiel Dror and Dana Kanze for allowing me to share your research.

To An Coppens, Jo Eckersley, Dame Jayne-Anne Gadhia DBE, FRSE and Charlotta Ginman for sharing your thoughts on what a brave new world might look like.

To Daniel Priestley for your input on the title of this book and for sharing your wisdom generously.

To my co-founders at Funding Focus Limited, Taryn April and Thibau Grumett, and our graphic designer, Jacob Furness.

To John van Kuffeler, my co-founder at Funding Focus Investment Trust plc, for your guidance, support and friendship over the past twenty years and your help in realising a dream; and to the rest of our board: our chair, Shalini Khemka CBE, Fran Boorman, Mehmuda Mian, Sophie Milliken and Julie Pomeroy.

To the team at Rethink Press: Lucy McCarraher, Joe Gregory, Kate Latham, Anke Ueberberg and especially Alison Jack, whose careful editing helped make the final version of the book so much better.

And to everyone else who has made a mark on my life. There are so many, and I thank you all.

The Author

David B Horne was born and raised on the west coast of Canada. He qualified as a Chartered Accountant with Price Waterhouse (now part of PwC) in 1987. Later that year, he and his wife moved to Zürich where David continued his career.

He left Price Waterhouse in 1989 and joined his largest client, NCR Switzerland, as financial controller. In 1993, David and his family moved from Zürich to London, where he continued with NCR. During this time, AT&T acquired NCR, and in 1995 he transferred to AT&T Capital. In 1997, David joined the BBC in his first finance director role. Three years later, he joined

BSMG Worldwide as CFO Europe, where he made his first business acquisitions, buying seven PR agencies in two years.

He launched his consultancy business, Add Then Multiply, in 2002 and ran it for a year before being appointed in 2003 as CFO of Huveaux plc, which was listed on London's Alternative Investment Market (AIM). In three years, he and the founder raised $84 million and bought eight companies, growing revenues 25× from $1.6 million to $40 million. He left in 2006 to become CFO of GoIndustry plc, which had just listed on AIM. There he raised $56 million and acquired a global competitor. In 2010, he resigned from GoIndustry.

At the end of 2010, David launched a wine business, Horne & Daughters, serving private clients and investing on Liv-ex, the London International Vintners Exchange. He also re-launched Add Then Multiply (http://addthenmultiply.com) and now works exclusively with entrepreneurs implementing his FACE methodology: fund, acquire, consolidate, exit. David has raised more than $140 million in debt and equity funding and bought or sold more than twenty companies.

In 2019, his book *Add Then Multiply: How small businesses can think like big businesses and achieve exponential growth* was published. It has since become an Amazon #1 bestseller and in March 2020 won the

Business Self Development category in the Business Book Awards (www.businessbookawards.co.uk).

He is founder of Funding Focus (www.funding-focus.com), a social enterprise whose mission is to level the uneven playing field which female and underrepresented entrepreneurs of all genders face when raising capital. Funding Focus is committed to supporting United Nations Sustainable Development Group (UNSDG) 4 – Quality Education – and UNSDG 5 – Gender Equality.

He is co-founder and CEO of Funding Focus Investment Trust plc, an investment trust in process of seeking a London Stock Exchange listing which intends to invest in and support female and underrepresented entrepreneurs (https://ffitplc.com).

He lives in London with his wife, Kate.

You can reach David on social media here:

in www.linkedin.com/in/david-b-horne

🐦 https://twitter.com/David_B_Horne

📷 https://instagram.com/DavidBHorne

Lightning Source UK Ltd.
Milton Keynes UK
UKHW021123050722
405396UK00004B/43